D1097983

Herzog
by Ebert

(Roger Ebert) Herzog
by Ebert

FOREWORD BY *Werner Herzog*

THE UNIVERSITY OF CHICAGO PRESS
Chicago and London

The University of Chicago Press, Chicago 60637
The University of Chicago Press, Ltd., London
© 2017 by The Ebert Company, Ltd.
Foreword © 2017 by The University of Chicago
University of Chicago Press, 1427 E. 60th St.,
Chicago, IL 60637.
Published 2017
Printed in the United States of America

26 25 24 23 22 21 20 19 18 17   1 2 3 4 5

ISBN-13: 978-0-226-50042-3   (cloth)
ISBN-13: 978-0-226-50056-0   (e-book)
DOI: 10.7208/chicago/9780226500560.001.0001

"'Images at the Horizon': A Workshop with Werner Herzog, Conducted by Roger Ebert at the Facets Multimedia Center, Chicago, Illinois, April 17, 1979, Transcribed, Annotated, and Edited by Gene Walsh" was originally published as a pamphlet by Facets Multimedia, Inc., © 1979, Facets Multimedia, Inc. Reprinted by permission of Facets Multimedia, Inc.

All other previously published reviews, essays, and interviews originally appeared in the *Chicago Sun-Times*, and are reprinted with permission. © Chicago Sun-Times, Inc., 1977, 1979, 1982, 1984, 1998–2000, 2002, 2005, 2007–2011, and 2013.

LIBRARY OF CONGRESS CATALOGING-IN-PUBLICATION DATA

Names: Ebert, Roger, author. | Herzog, Werner, 1942– writer of foreword.

Title: Herzog by Ebert / Roger Ebert ; foreword by Werner Herzog.

Description: Chicago ; London : The University of Chicago Press, 2017. | Includes index.

Identifiers: LCCN 2017003539 | ISBN 9780226500423 (cloth : alk. paper) | ISBN 9780226500560 (e-book)

Subjects: LCSH: Herzog, Werner, 1942– | Motion picture producers and directors.

Classification: LCC PN1998.3.H477 E24 2017 | DDC 791.4302/33092 — dc23 LC record available at https://lccn.loc.gov/2017003539

♾ This paper meets the requirements of ANSI/NISO Z39.48-1992 (Permanence of Paper).

Contents

Part 3: Interviews

Foreword

It would be incomplete if I just made a point that I am missing Roger Ebert. It goes far beyond him; it goes much deeper. Cinema, in rare cases, has created a few men and women we can consider the consciousness of all of us who love cinema, our guardians, our light at the end of the tunnel. Lotte Eisner was one of them, Amos Vogel as well, and so was Henri Langlios, the fierce dragon who guarded the treasures of cinema. Roger's and Lotte's and Henri's fire that they had within keeps us going. We would be lonesome stragglers left stranded in a cold and hostile world that knows no history and has no compass.

And this is the world Roger saw coming, and I saw coming, when the studio (Disney, I believe) left no doubt it wanted to take *At the Movies with Ebert and Roeper* in a "different" direction. What they meant, in blunt terms, was taking the show away from movie criticism and love and appreciation of cinema into the realm of celebrity news. This was not a singular shift. You saw it coming, as taking on Roeper meant accepting a partner who had hardly any clue about cinema, who had to be tutored in crash courses in what real cinema was all about. The print media, by now, have abandoned almost all of their film critics and replaced them with writers and paparazzi in hot pursuit of celebrities. The Internet, now, does the same.

I have never been part of what I call the culture of complaint, nor was Roger ever into this. He plowed on until there was no breath left in him. I always kept talking about him as the Good Soldier of Cinema, because he had started to call me exactly that, but I insisted, "Roger, this fits you much better." During the last decade of his life, he was a wonderful soldier, and I always admired him for his relentless bravery. When he passed away, a whole epoch expired with him. He had been the last remaining woolly mammoth.

What connected us? What brought us close to each other? It was Roger who was drawn to my films in the early seventies. He saw *Signs of Life*, my first feature film, and many of my early films that were hardly recognized by anyone. My film *Aguirre, the Wrath of God* ended up on his list of the ten best of all time, and a few others were included in his "Great Movies" series. This opened up the curiosity of wider American audiences. I owe him a lot. But it was not about that.

We did not meet very often. I can't even say we were real friends, because we did not see each other often enough. And both of us had the same feeling of caution: the reviewer and the filmmaker had to keep a respectful distance. We noticed this, I remember quite clearly, when one day Roger had a deep "soul talk" with me, speaking about his demons. I always had sensed that beneath the visible surface he was haunted, and there was a moment of almost shocking recognition that we should not go any further.

But we had a deep understanding about fundamental aspects of cinema, and art, if that does not sound too lofty. Today, we are experiencing a new "post-fact" and "alternative fact" world in politics. But we debated decades earlier aspects of fact and truth in cinema, and I was the one who postulated a form of cinema where facts did not necessarily constitute truth. Of course, no one can ignore facts—they have normative power—but in cinema we can experience a form of illumination, of "ecstatic" truth, that has been experienced by, among others, late medieval mystics. Why as we stand in front of Michelangelo's *Pieta* are we not cheated? Jesus, taken from the cross, is the tortured body of a man thirty-three years old, but his mother is seventeen. Did Michelangelo mislead us? No. He just gave us an essential truth about the Man of Sorrows, and his mother, the Virgin.

Reading the discourse at Facets Multimedia we had decades ago

(x)

makes me marvel at how much Roger and I have changed, and how much we have remained the same. It is a strange and wondrous blip in time to hear our voices so many years back.

I was asked at various occasions if his writing informed my films. No, it did not. Did the fact that we were cautious friends in any way change the course of my life? My answer is no again. But knowing him made it better.

Werner Herzog
January 2017

Editorial Note

Roger Ebert published his first review of a film directed by Werner Herzog—*Aguirre, the Wrath of God*—on February 9, 1977. His final piece concerning Herzog's work ("The Great Ecstasy of the Sculptor Herzog") appeared almost thirty-six years later, on January 26, 2013.

They met at the New York Film Festival in 1968, and, as Ebert notes in that final piece, "The first time I met him was at somebody's apartment in Greenwich Village. . . . I sat on the rug at his feet. What we talked about I have no idea, but I felt a strong connection and I've felt it ever since. He was a kid with a film at the festival, yet so much more than that."

This volume contains Ebert's reviews, interviews, "Great Movies" pieces, and other essays that explore that "strong connection." (See http://www.rogerebert.com/chazs-blog/rogers-favorites-werner-herzog for a guide to the Herzog material available at RogerEbert.com.) Also included is "Images at the Horizon," a transcript of the workshop featuring Werner Herzog that Roger Ebert conducted on April 17, 1979, at the Facets Multimedia Center in Chicago. It is a long discussion filled with fascinating insights about the first portion of Herzog's career. The appendix contains two items prepared for a retrospective of Herzog's work at the Walker Art Center in 1999—Ebert's brief note and Herzog's "Minnesota Declaration," which was presented at a question-and-answer session.

Although Ebert is not with us to provide the additional commentary that enhanced his other book about one director, *Scorsese by Ebert*, the following two statements suggest the deep respect and appreciation evident in this record of the long encounter between a major critic and the films of a major director.

From Ebert's introductory remarks at the Facets workshop: "To my mind, you are the most interesting director of the 1970s. Unlike so many others, instead of just returning again and again to the same subject matter and expressing it in exactly the same style, each of your films has been a *new* departure and provided us with a *new* vision."

From Ebert's letter of November 17, 2007, to Herzog: "I have started out to praise your work, and have ended by describing it. Maybe it is the same thing. You and your work are unique and invaluable, and you ennoble the cinema when so many debase it. You have the audacity to believe that if you make a film about anything that interests you, it will interest us as well. And you have proven it."

Here, then, are Ebert's words of description and praise and Herzog's words of explanation and clarification.

Part 1 Facets
Multimedia,
1979

Images at the Horizon

A workshop with Werner Herzog conducted by Roger Ebert at the Facets Multimedia
Center, Chicago, Illinois, April 17, 1979
(Transcribed, annotated, and edited by Gene Walsh in 1979, and with additional,
minor clarifications from Werner Herzog in 2017 indicated in brackets)

ROGER EBERT: I first saw your work at the 1968 New York Film Festival
when you brought *Signs of Life*, which was your first feature-length
film. You were a new name to us all at that time, and the New German Cinema itself was also very new, and now my personal opinion
is that in the last eleven years — I hope I don't embarrass you by
saying this — you have made the *most* interesting films given us by
any single director. To my mind, you are the most interesting director of the 1970s. Unlike so many others, instead of just returning
again and again to the same subject matter and expressing it in
exactly the same style, each of your films has been a *new* departure
and provided us with a *new* vision.

I think that one way to start this discussion tonight might be to
ask you to talk about the three films that were shown here today:
the feature-length documentary, *Land of Silence and Darkness*, and
the two shorter documentaries, *The Great Ecstasy of the Sculptor
Steiner* and *La Soufrière*. I had seen the two shorter documentaries
before, but tonight I saw *Land of Silence and Darkness* for the first
time, and it seemed to me that this film has a certain definite connection with *Kaspar Hauser: Every Man for Himself and God Against*

All. Both of these films seem to express your recognition of the fact that we *all* have a desperate need to communicate and that, in particular, a man—a person—who cannot speak and hear and talk and be understood is, in a very tragic way, completely closed off from existing as a human being.

WERNER HERZOG: Yes, it's true. I've always seen that very close connection between those two films. But I would also say *Land of Silence and Darkness* is very close to *Nosferatu* now, and it's very close to *Woyzeck*, and, of course, it's very close to *Stroszek* and to all the other films that I have made.

But *Land of Silence and Darkness* is a film that is particularly close to my heart because it is so pure. It's one of the *purest* films that I have ever made in the sense that it is one in which things are allowed to come across in the most direct way. The fact that it was made with a minimum of machinery and expense by just myself and one cinematographer, Schmidt-Reitwein, made possible this real difference in the directness of its approach.

Another reason that I like to show this film to more intimate audiences like this is because I would like that it should be a source of encouragement for all of you who want to make films. This particular film was made on less than thirty thousand dollars. You should know that you can make films like this almost without any money at all. You can make a film just with the guts, just with the sense that you *have* to make it. In fact, you can make a film like this for *no* money at all! You only have to steal, let's say, fifty thousand feet of raw stock, expropriate a camera for two weeks, and that's it! (LAUGHTER FROM AUDIENCE.)

And so that's another of the reasons why I like to show this film.

Besides, when we tried to figure out the details of my stay here, I personally asked Milos Stehlik, the Director of Facets, and the people at New Yorker Films, who distribute most of my films in this country, to arrange to show some of my documentaries, because they are almost always neglected by the public, and yet for me they are just as important as my feature films. There is something in *Land of Silence and Darkness* that is almost like a part of me, but

I would say that a film like *The Great Ecstasy of the Sculptor Steiner* is a film which is also very close to me in a slightly different way. In *Steiner* the reasons for this feeling of closeness are, perhaps, even clearer, more nearly at the surface, because it's almost an autobiographical film. At one time I wanted to become a world champion in ski jumping myself, and I think it is only because I quit my career as a ski jumper at the age of sixteen that I then really started to make films.

RE: When exactly did you start to make films? You must have started very early. You're thirty-six years old now, and so your film, *Signs of Life*, must have been made when you were only twenty-four, and I understand that you made four short films even before that! Could you tell us something about those films?

(5)

WH: I started to make films very early. At the age of fourteen or fifteen it was already quite clear to me, apart from becoming a ski jumper, that I was going to make films. But, of course, I had many years of failures and humiliations. I did all the things that everyone does who tries to make films and doesn't really know what the business is all about: I submitted my projects to several producers and to various television stations and so on . . . and *all* of them were rejected. It was very humiliating how these people kicked me out of their offices.

But finally when I was seventeen and a half or almost eighteen . . .

RE: When you were *sixteen*, the networks weren't interested in you?

(LAUGHTER FROM AUDIENCE.)

WH: No, it's not like that because by that time I had already submitted one project—it was on reforms in penitentiaries—that those people actually liked very much. They said that they really wanted to make the film, but, since I had had such bad experiences in showing up myself, because I was still a schoolboy, I didn't want to walk into their office. I just made phone calls, and I wrote letters to them. I even had some letterhead printed to make myself look more impressive. Then, after two months of negotiations—because I wanted to direct the film myself—it was inevitable that I had to see them, and, when I finally walked into their office, a secretary opened the door, and they just looked *beyond* me as if expecting to see the father that had come with his boy!

(LAUGHTER FROM AUDIENCE.)

But, of course, there was no one behind me. All this lasted only ten seconds, and then the whole thing was over, but it made me very mad. Because these people had made such rude and insipid remarks, I thought to myself, "For heaven's sake, what made *them* 'producers,' these assholes?"

(LAUGHTER FROM AUDIENCE.)

How did *these* people become producers?

Out of this experience, I discovered that I would never be able to make a film in my whole life if I did not become a producer myself, and so the very same night I started to work in a factory—a steel factory—doing welding, and I did that for two years from eight o'clock at night until six in the morning. During the daytime I was still in school, but in the evenings [working the night shifts] I was able to make enough money to produce my first three short films.

RE: Was your first film shot in 35 mm?

WH: Yes, I started shooting with 35 mm film immediately.

RE: What were the subjects of your first films?

WH: My first film, *Herakles*, is a film that I do not like very much. I like *all* my films, but there are two among them that I really do not like that much. *Herakles* was only a sort of test for me in terms of learning how to edit very diversified materials. It's a film on bodybuilding, but it's just too superficial for me to be able to call it a *real* film on bodybuilding or anything else.

Then I made *Game in the Sand* in 1962. Only three or four people have seen it so far, and I really would not want to call this a "film." Not as long as I live!

And then I made *Precautions against Fanatics* and *Last Words*, but *Last Words*, a short film that I like *very* much, is a film which was made during the shooting of *Signs of Life*. I had written the screenplay for *Signs of Life* when I was nineteen, but it took me *four* years until I got all the finances together for it. So it was a very, very long hard struggle.

RE: In terms of the films that you have made since then, *Signs of Life* is a rather traditional film in style, isn't it?

WH: No, I don't agree. It only looks on the surface as if it were made in a traditional style, but, in fact, it's really a film that is unique in that it has complete innocence. It's my only innocent film. This kind of innocence is something like virginity that is over when once you do it.

RE: In other words, since *Signs of Life* was a film that you made without having made another feature, you were able to be completely fresh in your approach toward making it.

WH: No, it's something else. Even today I still am able to approach each film in a fresh way. It's something else. For example, when I see my films in a retrospective—and recently I saw *Signs of Life* in just this sort of a series—I always have the very strong feeling that this particular film is my *only* really innocent film. It was made somehow as if there were not film history. Something like that happens only once in your lifetime, because, when once you have lost this innocence by doing your first film, or maybe your second, or third, then you . . .

RE: Then you become *aware* of yourself as an artist.

WH: No, but I think we should leave it at that. I cannot explain it any better.

RE: Your next film was *Fata Morgana*?

WH: Yes.

RE: That was a film that when it was first shown in this country—I don't know what kind of reception it got overseas—but it got a very hostile press in New York in particular.

WH: Almost everywhere.

RE: I remember at that time all the people who loved *Signs of Life*— when you came back to the New York Film Festival with *Fata Morgana*—they said, "Here is this promising young director— this brilliant director from Germany—why does he make such an

(7)

inaccessible film? Why doesn't he want to make a film that people will want to come to see?"

WH: But it is *not* inaccessible. I found that out, and I told those people immediately, ten years ago, that they would soon get acquainted with this kind of filmmaking, and I think that it has all worked out that way now. After ten years, that film is *still* alive—still people go and see it—and they understand it *much* better now, I think.

It's very strange, but people always have certain expectations. They want me to do certain things that are just in their own minds. They do not see that I also have my needs and my anxieties and my fascinations. Then, for instance, when I come up with a film like *Nosferatu*—a *vampire* film—everyone starts to wonder just why I should want to make a vampire film, as if they just cannot believe it, and yet this film is *so* close to everything else that I have made so far!

You know it's very, very difficult for anyone to continue to work in this medium, because there's *always* some sort of public opinion or public expectation which interferes in some way. If I had followed up *all* the public expectations or even just the expectations of the press, I think I wouldn't have been able to make *any* films at all anymore!

Once in a while—very often, in fact—I have thought to myself, "Why are all these people so mad? Why are they so insane? Why don't they just accept what I do? Why not just come and have a look at it?" But instead they are always coming toward my work with plans for certain sorts of "prefabricated houses" already in their minds, and for some reason they expect that my work should follow exactly the pattern of those prefabricated mobile homes which they happen to have sticking somewhere in their brains.

RE: And, if we've seen *Stroszek*, we know you could never really count on a mobile home!

(LAUGHTER FROM AUDIENCE.)

But, if I were asked, and I have not been asked, so I will just, you know, kind of subtly ask myself, and then answer to the question, "What is the connection between *Nosferatu* and your other films in terms of both subject and theme?" My answer to this would be that in many of your films—both your fictional films and your documentaries—you seem to show a fascination with characters who live at an *extreme* of life. This could be either an extreme personal experience that is *chosen* or an extreme position that is *forced* upon them by circumstances: by a handicap, for example, or by cruel behavior, or by just their inherent oddness. However, when I suggested to you earlier that this was something that I saw again and again in your films—people living at the edge of life or at the extremes of existence—you said that this interpretation was somehow too simple.

WH: Yes, because I think that what you say carries with it an understanding, let's say, of a figure such as Kaspar Hauser, that he was something odd, or something marginal, or something bizarre, or something extreme. But, when you take a look at the film, you will find out very soon that Kaspar is the *only* one who makes sense, the *only* one who is dignified, who has a radical human dignity—and all the rest are insane and bizarre and eccentric. Yes, all the rest are eccentric! And I think that individuals like Kaspar Hauser are not so much "marginal" figures. They are just very *pure* figures that have somehow been able to survive in a more or less pure form. Sometimes, of course, they are under very heavy pressure, like, let's say, Steiner,[1] or like Fini Straubinger,[2] or even like myself when I was making *La Soufrière*. But, under this sort of pressure, people reveal their various natures to us. It's exactly the same that is done in chemistry when you have a particular substance that is unknown to you. When this happens, you must put this substance under extreme conditions—like extreme heat, extreme pressure, extreme radiation—and it is only *then* that you will be able to find out the essential structure of this substance which you are trying to explain and to discover and to describe.

RE: That, in a sense, is what happened in *Aguirre, the Wrath of God.*

WH: In almost *all* of the films.

RE: So, perhaps, when I'm saying that your characters are at extremes, it doesn't necessarily mean that they themselves are "extreme" objectively, but only that they are in an *extreme* relationship to the

(9)

society that they find themselves in. Kaspar Hauser, for example, is very much an outsider as he is seen by everybody else who is alive at that time in that particular society.

WH: But he's *not* an outsider: he is the very center, and all the rest are outsiders! That's the point of the film.

I don't know exactly how many of you in this country also think that Kaspar is some kind of a bizarre strange figure, but, if you do, it's exactly the same thing that has happened with audiences, for example, in Germany. There's so much hatred there against my films that you probably wouldn't even believe it. *Aguirre* got by far the worst reviews that I've seen in ten years for *any* film, and now for *Nosferatu* it's still going on and on. In Germany, in my *own* country, people have tried to label me personally as an eccentric, as some sort of strange freak that does not fit into any of their patterns. And that's ridiculous. *They* are insane!

(LAUGHTER FROM AUDIENCE, FOLLOWED BY APPLAUSE.)

RE: I was rather shocked when you told me that *Aguirre* ran for only three weeks in Munich, which is your home city, and then moved to another theater where it only ran for one additional week. Later, when people there said, "Well, why can't we see it?" you told them that they all could have seen it if only they had given it the proper support. Did you know that *Aguirre* even had a longer run than that right here in Chicago?

WH: Yes.

RE: To begin with, I think, there was a built-in resistance on the part of Chicago audiences — and even American audiences in general — to films from Germany from directors that they had not yet heard about, but then an educational process went forward. Places like Facets[3] and the Film Festival[4] and the Film Center[5] began to show all these interesting new *German* films — I'm stressing this point because I think it's generally agreed that many of the most interesting films of the last ten years have been coming out of Germany — with the eventual result that an audience has now developed to the point where your films *do* play here commercially, and while they don't make as much money as they do in Rome, for example, where your *Nosferatu* has just broken the house record recently set by *Grease*, and while we realize that that degree of commercial success is probably *not* going to happen in Chicago for quite a few years, nevertheless, the turnout here tonight, for example, and the successful commercial runs of your films in this city would seem to indicate that you are not considered by us to be quite as "bizarre," shall we say, as you are in Germany.

WH: Yes, that's true, and it's also true that during this time my only means of survival has been on the basis of showings of my films *outside* of Germany, like in Algeria or in Mexico or in France or in Yugoslavia or here in the United States. In Germany I have had to work for eleven years in almost a total void, without any response at all. There was *some* response, of course, from a small flock of friends and believers who would come to see *all* my films—but, although you can write books or do paintings for ten or eleven years without having any sizable public response, for me to be able to survive in filmmaking for so long has been a complete miracle. I do not fully understand how I have managed to survive all this time, but probably the most important factor in my survival has been the reception of my films outside Germany—particularly in the United States—which has grown more and more through the years. That you are here now and that you are looking at my films is the basis for my survival, and it has been the basis for my survival for at least a decade. That's why I like to come here. I have no other specific reason for coming here. Usually I would much rather go to more remote places. Chicago is very big, and I would prefer to go to smaller places which are, like Mongolia, still unexplored.

RE: Unfortunately there are whole states in the United States where a subtitled film has never yet been played commercially.

WH: Yes, it's a great problem for many people here in this country to accept a culture that is not their own, because this country still is struggling very hard just to define its own cultures. It has so many roots and so many different ethnic minorities, and they all are still in a process of amalgamation. What this means is that whenever something comes toward them from outside, they will

(11)

always try to keep their "fences" completely closed. So it really is not surprising that it sometimes takes very, very long in order to jump those fences!

RE: You might want to say something about your theory that Americans are, in fact, much more bizarre than they believe.

WH: Another thing about Americans that I've said before is that these people here believe that they are normal, that they make sense, and that the *rest* of the world is exotic. They do not seem to understand that they are the *most* exotic people in the world right now. Believe me, I say this with a *lot* of sympathy!

(LAUGHTER FROM AUDIENCE.)

I have been in the United States a couple of times now, and every single time I come here I'm surprised all over again. In San Francisco, for example, I switched on the television, and there was this preacher who for *four* hours was screaming for money! Without even a break for commercials!

(LAUGHTER FROM AUDIENCE.)

And that's not an event that only takes place somewhere in California. This program is broadcast nationwide! His name, I think, is Scott, a white-haired . . .

RE: Did you get his address?

WH: No, but there are many wonderful preachers all around and I like them *very* much! I would like to get in closer touch with them.

RE: Was this sort of vision of the United States one of the main reasons why you wanted to make *Stroszek* and your documentary on auctioneers, *How Much Wood Would a Woodchuck Chuck?*

WH: The film about auctioneers is something quite different. It's about discovering the *ultimate* language—the very last poetry that is ultimately imaginable—and about just how far language itself can go in this capitalistic system. Every single system develops its own sort of *extreme* language. For example, in Germany we've developed the language of propaganda to a still unchallenged extreme. Or, for another example, the Orthodox Church has developed the use of ritual chant in their liturgy in a way that is also unparalleled and quite extreme. And now this capitalistic society has begun to

(12)

develop its own sort of an ultimate language, which is, for me, the language of the auctioneers!

RE: What's fascinating though is that you would want to make a film about somebody who talks as fast as it is possible to talk and yet still want to make other films about people who do not talk at all and cannot even hear or see.

WH: But with the auctioneers it's not *only* talking fast. It's almost like a ritualistic incantation. It has a common borderline with the last poetry that is possible for us, and it is very close to music as well.

But, anyway, *Stroszek* goes more vitally into what I'm concerned with, because in Western Europe, in particular, there is *such* a strong domination of American culture and American films! And *all* of us who are working in filmmaking have to deal with this sort of domination. For me, it was particularly important to define my position about this country and its culture, and that's one of the major reasons I made *Stroszek*.

But another important reason for making *Stroszek* was that I originally wanted to make a film of *Woyzeck* with Bruno. *Woyzeck*, you know, is a subject that goes back to a theater fragment by a German poet, Georg Büchner, who died in 1837. He was probably the *most* ingenious writer for the stage that we ever had, and Büchner, who unfortunately died at the age of twenty-three, left his drama *Woyzeck* unfinished, as just a fragment. Nobody even knows for certain the exact sequence of his scenes, but, even so, it's extraordinary! It's really the most remarkable and probably the strongest drama text that has ever been written in the German language, and I wanted to make this text into a film with Bruno. But then I had some afterthoughts, and I had the feeling that it was *not* Bruno who should be the one to play in *Woyzeck*, and so I told him, "Bruno, I'm going to invent a story for you, not a *Woyzeck* but something with a basic feeling like *Woyzeck* in it." And so I wrote *Stroszek*, although *Woyzeck* was still on my mind, and it still kept on bothering me.

Then last year, right after I shot *Nosferatu*, the vampire film, only five days later, I shot *Woyzeck* with the same crew and the same leading actor, Klaus Kinski, who is known to you as "Aguirre." But now the situation is such that you will probably see *Woyzeck before* you will see *Nosferatu* here in this country.

RE: Since you mentioned Bruno S., who is the person who plays "Kaspar Hauser" and who also, of course, is the star of *Stroszek*, perhaps you could talk to us a little bit about your use of Bruno and his feelings about being in movies and what you describe as his "twenty-three years in captivity."

WH: Well, when you ask me about the *use* of Bruno . . .

RE: Or the *collaboration* with him, I should have said.

WH: Yes, but still that always implies a question of morality.

RE: I didn't intend . . .

WH: And, when one speaks about the *use* of Bruno, it always sounds like an accusation, and so I will take it as that!

(LAUGHTER FROM AUDIENCE.)

Yes, because to make a film with a man like him always has a question of morality involved, and, I think, this was the all-pervading problem that we were aware of during the shooting of both the films that we made with him.

Perhaps I have to explain a little bit about Bruno so that you can understand. He was born as an illegitimate child to a prostitute in Berlin, and she really did not want to have a baby so she used to beat him. Then, when he was three, she beat him so hard that he lost his power of speech, and this was a perfect pretext for her to put him away into an asylum for retarded children, a place where he *definitely* did not belong. He was very much afraid of being in this situation because the other children in that place were either insane or extremely retarded, and he was *quite* smart. So, at the age of nine, after six years of captivity in there, he started trying to escape, but then, when he finally did escape, he was captured and put into a correctional institution. From there he escaped again and again, and each time he was put into more and more severe correctional institutions. Eventually he developed a long record of minor criminal offenses: for example, for vagrancy or public indecency. One of these times he broke into a car in wintertime when it was snowing, and he slept inside the car. Next morning the police dragged him out, and for this he was given a five months' term in prison. And so, all together, he was forced to spend a total of twenty-three years in this kind of captivity, and, as a result, in many ways he's been almost completely destroyed. By the time I met him, he was really as badly mutilated as any man I have ever seen in all my life, but, even so, in terms of making a film with him, once you have decided to make that film—or *any* film, for that matter—on the very bottom line of things, it must always be an exchange of services. It's always an exchange of *using* each other for the sake of a particular project, for the realization of a certain film that we have decided to make together. Bruno knew that each of us—myself as much as anyone else—would have to submit our private feelings and our laziness and our personal desires to that final goal that we all had together. I think that Bruno understood this completely.

One signal for me that he understood all this—one particular thing that was very significant for me—was that for the entire six weeks of shooting for *Kaspar Hauser* he did not even once take off his costume. He actually slept in his costume all the time. In the little town where we shot that film we were staying in a hotel, but, since Bruno was always in a situation in which he believed that he might need to escape and run away immediately, he never slept in the bed. It was really very pathetic [full of human pathos]. He just had a pillow and a blanket on the ground right next to the exit door.

On another occasion I also spent some time with him in his own apartment. Here we slept in the same room, but one day I had to get up very early at 5:30 in the morning while Bruno was still there snoring, and so, before leaving, I said, "Bruno," very quietly to him to tell him that I was going. His reaction to this was so pathetic [deeply filled with tragedy]. It was just as if you had hit him with a bullet. He jumped right out of that bed and was standing there, and he said, "Yes!" just as if he were going to have to run.

Really, things like that are *so* tragic that, of course, it is a very, very important question whether or not one should ever make a

(15)

film with him at all or just keep your hands off entirely. But, in this particular instance, I think Bruno understood that this was also going to be a film *about* him, that it was also going to be a way of revealing his own situation to him. It was a way of making things more "transparent" to him, and I think he understood that. But he also understood that six weeks of shooting a film could never repair all the damages that already had been done to him.

Still there remains a very, very deep loneliness in that man and a basic distrust of *any* human being. Even so, there were sometimes signals of trust. For example, when he would want to be very affectionate but could not express it directly in words, he would come and grab and squeeze my fingertip. But, then, the very next moment he would accuse me of stealing his salary away from him simply because I had opened a bank account for him. I had even asked him before to do this for himself. The reason that I had tried to talk him into doing this was because at night, when he would go to a bar, he would just get himself drunk and toss his money around so that by the next morning he would always have spent all of his salary. That's why we opened this bank account for him, but he thought there was a big conspiracy going on between me and the boss of that bank to steal the money back from him again. So one day I asked the boss of the bank to have lunch with us so that he could explain to Bruno that there was no conspiracy, and this man tried for *two* hours to explain to Bruno that only he himself with his own signature could withdraw any money from that account whenever he wished to do so, but Bruno *still* wouldn't believe it. So we took all the money out, and we left it in his closet! But I understand that he finally keeps his own bank account now, that he finally trusts in it.

I also know that he is *still* obsessed with death. For example, his greatest obsession during the shooting of *Kaspar Hauser* involved his scene in the morgue with that big stone table. He wanted to *have* that table! He always said to me, "This is the table of truth, because we are *all* going to end up here stark naked, and no one will be any different." This was the table of truth for Bruno, but it weighed almost a ton, and so we couldn't buy it. Finally I bought him a table out of a surgery room which had flexible parts all over it—a *really* wonderful one!—and he keeps it now in his apartment.

Yes, now his situation has somewhat improved. He has moved into a three-room apartment which you can see for yourself in the film *Stroszek*. Yes, part of that film was shot in his own apartment, and there you will see the piano, for example, which he bought with his salary from *Kaspar Hauser*. So his personal conditions have improved slightly, but not drastically, because he's still doing a job in a steel factory in Berlin. He has never quit that job. We only shot these two films during his vacations.

RE: You told me earlier that Bruno to this day in Germany is actually better known as a street musician than as a film personality.

WH: That only pertains to the situation in Berlin where he lives and where he's been a street singer for twelve years. He knows by now every single backyard in Berlin, and all the people there also know him. I only mentioned this to you because I wanted you to know that in making our film it was not so much a question of us just dragging him out into the light in front of cameras. By the time that the film was made, he had already been a public figure in Berlin making appearances in front of small crowds in backyards for at least a dozen years. So it really was not so shocking for him to be in a film. Besides, he had already been in a film before this, a semidocumentary by a young Berlin filmmaker, an excellent movie called *Bruno the Black*.[6] That, in fact, is how I discovered him.

RE: When you said that you spent ten years making films without having very much financial support or even developing very much of a following in Germany, I was going to ask you if it was particularly difficult to finance films when you have a fairly unpredictable person in the lead like Bruno, but, then, it occurred to me that you would probably *never* make a film that was easy to finance because, in addition to the difficulties that are often inherent in filmmaking, you *always* make films which seem to be almost impossible to make anyway: for example, *Aguirre, the Wrath of God*.

WH: Yes, people in some of the studios have asked me, "How, for heaven's sake, could you possibly have produced that film your-self? It must have cost $5 million at least!" Then, when I told them that it was made for only $320,000, they simply didn't believe me. They just thought I was a liar. They *still* do not believe me, but it's the truth!

Here in this country you always have the inclination to speak about money, as if money in itself could ever produce a film! As if money had *ever* moved a mountain. It is *never* money that moves a mountain!

RE: Not money, but will.

WH: No, it's more than that. It's faith or spirit—people who fight for their lives—or just sheer guts! But it has never been cash money that's made my films. Of course, cash money has always been involved—it's like some sort of "grease" that keeps things going—but it's only one of the several components that go into making films. It is *never* money alone that makes films. It is not money that moves a mountain!

WORKSHOP MEMBER #1: You told us where you found Bruno, but where did you find the actors who play the various Americans in *Stroszek?* Were they *all* from Wisconsin?

WH: Yes, I found them *all* in Plainfield, Wisconsin, which is called "Railroad Flats" in the film, but, as a matter of fact, "Railroad Flats" is really this place named Plainfield, Wisconsin, a little town of 480 people. In this place, within five years, *eight* of these people became mass murderers!

(EXCLAMATIONS OF SURPRISE AND SOME LAUGHTER FROM AUDIENCE.)

And the most notorious case—one which you might have heard about—was Ed Gein, the man who decapitated and skinned people and made a throne seat out of human flesh and other things like that! He was a man from Plainfield, Wisconsin.

I went there with a friend of mine, Errol Morris, who has now made an excellent film. This is his first film, and it is called *Gates of Heaven.* Try to see that film! Did you know that I had to push him very hard in order to get him to make that film? It was the type of situation where he was always complaining to me that he had no money to make a film, and so I finally said to him, "You just don't have the guts to do it!" I even said, "But, if you *do* start to make your film tomorrow, I'm going to eat my shoes!"—and I *did* so! (LAUGHTER FROM AUDIENCE.)

That's why I'm wearing new boots today!

But, anyway, Errol Morris had been investigating all these murder cases for two years, and he had about five thousand pages of transcripts. Really incredible stuff! But the reason that I ended up in Plainfield, Wisconsin, was because of one particular question that had arisen from all this research. He had found out that Ed Gein had also dug up graves—it's rather well-known, this fact—but, in addition, he had also found out that all these dug-up graves made a perfect circle and that the very center of this circle was the grave of Ed Gein's mother! So naturally we were *very* curious to find out if he had also excavated the body of his own mother, and the only real way to find out the answer to this was by going at night and digging in that graveyard!

So, after I had completed some shooting in Alaska for *Heart of Glass*, we made an appointment to meet at a certain date down in Plainfield, Wisconsin.

RE: Did he *really* dig up his mother?

WH: I don't know, because we never ended up digging in that graveyard, and I'll tell you why. It was because my friend did not show up! Of course, I was very much interested in finding out the answer myself, but I would not do it alone. It was primarily Errol Morris's own battle to find this answer out. So, when he did not show up, I called him and said, "I think it is good that we did not do it, because, sometimes, it is better and more valuable to have an *open* question than to have one that is answered. To have to keep this question open—did he really dig up his mother or not?—and not knowing is *much* more exciting and *much* more rewarding than simply knowing the real answer."

So, now, I think it was good that he was such a mess and did not show up, but, when he didn't show up, at *that* time, our car had

(19)

broken down in Plainfield, Wisconsin, and there was no garage anywhere around. We asked people if there was anyone there who could help us, and they all said, "Yes, there's a wreckage yard just a mile outside of town." So we went there, and there was this man, and I liked him *so* much . . .

(LAUGHTER FROM AUDIENCE.)

But that wreckage yard itself was so sad with all these ducks sitting around in the cold, and this man who owned it had an Indian [Native American] assistant whom he used to shout at and kick in the ass!

Then, a year later, when I came back to film *Stroszek*, I found him again, and I said, "I want to make a movie here. Where is your assistant, that Indian who works for you?" and he said, "What Indian?" He didn't even remember the Indian because he had hired that guy for one day and was so dissatisfied with him that he had fired him that very same evening. He didn't even remember at first that he had ever hired that man once! But we finally tracked that Indian down.

WORKSHOP MEMBER #2: In *Stroszek*, those two people on their tractors carrying guns—was that really happening out there?

WH: No, that was invented, but actually something like that might have happened at any moment. It is really very dangerous there in Plainfield, because those people are all so trigger-happy that sometimes they will just shoot instantly at whatever moves. So, you see, it was probably a really good thing that we did not dig in that graveyard there, because, if they had seen us in the graveyard digging, they might not have asked questions but just opened fire!

During the filming of *Stroszek*, even then, there were several serious shooting incidents because it was the hunting season. As you may know, each season there are some 250,000 hunters that come up to this area for deer hunting.

During this time, I had asked my editor Beate Mainka-Jellinghaus to come with us to location. She was so fed up with just sitting all the time in the editing room that finally I said to her, "Please come with us and do continuity." But, when she got there, it was so *extremely* cold that she decided to wear this reindeer coat which came all the way down to her ankles, and, wearing this coat, she was just walking across an open field when suddenly a police car stopped, and these two cops rushed out and jumped her, just like on a football field! They brought her down to the ground because they were quite convinced that if she had walked another fifty yards she would have been shot!

Did you know that *every* year in that town they shoot about fifteen people and that they also shoot about 150 cows!

(LAUGHTER FROM AUDIENCE.)

And do you know in Plainfield, Wisconsin, what the farmers do? With white oil paint, they write on their animals in great big letters: C O W. This is a *cow*!

(LAUGHTER FROM AUDIENCE.)

Oh, it's a *wonderful* place!

(LAUGHTER FROM AUDIENCE.)

Well, you would like it there. You know there are some of these places in the United States where all the lines of force somehow cross each other almost like knots, like a certain sort of concentration of what's going on in the rest of the United States. These are places like the stock exchange on Wall Street, like San Quentin Prison, like Disneyland, like Las Vegas . . . and like Plainfield, Wisconsin! Please remember that town!

RE: I realize I probably shouldn't ask this question, but which of your films do you think is your best film? Is it *Aguirre* or *Even Dwarfs Started Small* or, perhaps, *Heart of Glass*?

WH: I never speak about my *best* film. I really like them *all* very much, with the exception of the first two which I do not like that much. I like them *all* like children. Children are never perfect, and they all have their weaknesses and their strong points, but what matters is that they are *alive*. All these films are still very much alive so I wouldn't be able to give a preference to any individual one. Even so, however, I do have the feeling that a film like *Even Dwarfs Started Small* is going to outlive *Aguirre*. It's going to become older. Just as you might predict that, since this particular child is not very strong physically, as a man he will probably not grow older than—let's say—sixty, whereas another child may live to become ninety, so, in a similar way, I think that *Dwarfs* will outlive *Aguirre*, but, then again, maybe I am wrong.

RE: I'm handicapped at this point because *Even Dwarfs Started Small* is one of the few films that you have made that I have never seen, but I would like to say that I do find *Heart of Glass* to be terrifically moving, profoundly mysterious and poetic.

WH: Thank you for saying that, because this film, in particular, has had *very* bad press here in this country. [Maybe because it was so unprecedented to see a film with all its actors under hypnosis.]

RE: It made *every* ten-best list here in Chicago.

WH: Yes, but, generally speaking, it is *still* one of those films that has not been accepted, particularly not here in this country, and I like that film very much because I learned so much from having made it.

During the many preliminary tests we arranged before we shot *Heart of Glass*, we saw many interesting examples of just how extremely well memory works under hypnosis. One of the most fascinating things that I learned is the extent to which people can bring out something that is hidden very deep inside and perform it publicly in their state of trance.

But now I have gone beyond that. For example, I have shown films to audiences already under hypnosis. In order to accomplish this, I went to a theater and instructed all the people there that I would show a film to them, and that, if they wished, they could experience this film under hypnosis. This way I discovered that, if you look at a film under hypnosis, you *may* be able to have visionary experiences of a type that you have never had before. Of course, it does not work in exactly the same way with everyone. There are a lot of variations. In fact, every single person saw the film in a different way, but I would say that 30 percent of the people who saw the film under hypnosis had absolutely unique visionary experiences.

One purpose of this experiment in hypnosis was to discover to what extent it would be possible to bring out and emphasize those "poetic" visionary qualities that are hidden inside so many people. So, in order to find out just how inventive they really were, I hypnotized them. First I told them, "You are an inventor of great genius, and you are working on an insane, beautiful invention," and then I told them, "Invent now, and, when I come to you and put my hand on your shoulder, you will tell me what you are inventing, exactly what sort of machinery it is that you have created." And the results were so incredible that you just wouldn't even believe it! So much imagination, it was just incredible!

And then I tried to provoke poetic language out of people who had never before even been in touch with any kind of poetry. But you know you cannot simply say to them, "Now you are a great poet." If you were to do this, they would not become great poets. They would not even be able to write or produce a single line of poetry. It's always a question of *how* you suggest it to them. So, in this instance, what I suggested to them was that they were traveling into a strange, exotic, beautiful country with forms of jungle, birds, and trees that they had never seen before in all their lives and that for the first time they were going to set foot on an island which had not been visited for hundreds of years. And I told them that, when they were walking through this jungle, they would come across a huge rock and that, when they took a closer look, they would see that this was not just an ordinary rock but was instead one solid, smooth piece of emerald. And I told them that there was a poet five hundred years ago—a holy monk who had lived on this island and who was a *great* poet—and he had left an inscription on this rock. It took him all of his life to carve this inscription because the emerald was so hard. It took him all of his life to engrave with a chisel and a hammer this one single poem on the rock. And then I told them, "Now, when I put my hand on your shoulder, you will open your eyes, and you will be the first one who is privileged to see and read this poem." And so I put my hand on the shoulder of a man who was at least fifty-five years old and who was working in a horse stable—a stable cleaner without *any* formal education—and this man started to "read" a poem that was really very beautiful. With a very strange voice, he started to recite, and here is what he said: "Why can't we drink the moon? Why is there no vessel to hold it?" And it went on and on like this, and it was very, very beautiful.

But, after that, I decided to stop doing these tests because I did not have a clear enough idea of exactly what I was going to study, and tests of this kind should be done very carefully and cautiously because they also imply certain definite risks.

At the present time, I think that we do not know very much about the process of vision itself. We know *so* very little about it, and, with this kind of experimental work that I have been describing, we might soon be able to learn a little bit more. This kind of knowledge is precisely what we *need*. We need it very urgently because we live in a society that has *no* adequate images anymore, and, if we do not find adequate images and an adequate language for our civilization with which to express them, we will die out like the dinosaurs. It's as simple as that! We have already recognized that problems like the energy shortage or the overpopulation of the world or the environmental crisis are great dangers for our society and for our kind of civilization, but I think it has not yet been understood widely enough that we also absolutely *need* new images.

WORKSHOP MEMBER #3: In relation to your statement about new images, I've recently seen *Nosferatu* in a prerelease screening, and I believe that *Fata Morgana*, *Heart of Glass*, and *Nosferatu* are your most fully realized films in terms of what you believe about the importance of creating new images. I was wondering if possibly you feel the same way?

WH: To some extent, yes, but I think that this same striving—this *trying* to articulate new images—is present in *all* my films.

One should never attempt to define this process *just* in terms of the images that you see on the screen, because it also involves a new form of "emotionality" which somehow underlies the images in *all* these films. For example, if all of you had not seen *Land of Silence and Darkness* and if I were to show you only the last five minutes of the film—the scene where there's a man who embraces a tree—all of you would probably think, "Well, there's a man who embraces a tree," and that's all. What's happening is really very simple: you just see a man who feels and embraces a tree, and that *is* all, but, if you had seen the *entire* film, then you would have received this scene and this image with a different dimension of depth and insight. It requires that additional one and a half hours of film preceding this scene to make you receptive and sensitive enough to be able to understand that this is one of the deepest moments you can ever encounter in the cinema.

So, you see, it's not *just* the image itself which conveys this meaning, but it's *very* hard to verbalize exactly what I mean. Perhaps, since you seem to have some sympathy for my films, you will also be able to understand what I mean, but I know I cannot really teach this to you. I cannot teach you. You have to see it for yourself. You have to be able to sense it directly. That is why the films count much more than anything I could possibly tell you. It's misleading to have me here and have all this attention focused on me personally because the *only* thing that really counts is what you see on the screen.

Neither do I want to take the privilege away from you of discovering certain things for yourself nor do I want to "squeeze" into you certain opinions of my own—yet it has happened very often to me that, when I've tried to verbalize and to explain on a very personal level what I meant to express in my films, people take me like Moses—like a prophet of some sort—and then they say, "Well, but the films don't fulfill exactly what he says. They just don't make sense the way he says they do." Very often—very, very often, in fact—I have run into trouble of this kind because what I say often does not seem to make sense for people in respect to the films that they have seen. Therefore, I hesitate at this time—or *any* time—to give you a "recipe" for understanding them.

WORKSHOP MEMBER #4: I also saw a prerelease screening of the ninety-four minute American version of *Nosferatu*, and I noticed that several scenes are missing which were described in articles about the production of the film—such as, for example, a certain scene with Clemens Scheitz that shows him spreading the plague

(25)

and also a scene where Klaus Kinski as "Nosferatu" frightens horses that are on the horizon just by making a slight gesture—and I was wondering if there is a different length or slightly different content in the German language version and if there is any way that we will be able to see *that* version?

WH: Yes, what you have read is true. These scenes do, in fact, exist, but they were never part of the completed film, neither in the German nor in the English version. As you seem to know, we shot the film in two languages, in German and in English, and both versions are slightly different from each other, but in substance they are the same. The two scenes that you have mentioned were left out of *both* versions in very early stages of the editing.

Both these scenes in and of themselves were very beautiful, particularly the scene where the vampire frightens the horses: in this scene there are some horses grazing on the meadow, and he just stands there and very slowly raises his arm, and he has long claws, and he only does just *that* and the horses go off in panic! We had an explosive device behind the camera, of course, with the fuse set to go off at the very moment he does that, and this scene looked very good on the screen, but, in context with the scene that was shown right before, it looked too much like a circus trick, and, in the context of the entire film, I didn't like it anymore.

Now, in regard to your question about the scene involving Clemens Scheitz, there are actually *two* scenes that I cut out which are also very good scenes in themselves, and I've even shot certain other longer sequences that are entirely cut out of the final version of the film.

Exactly the same thing has happened to *all* my films. In *Aguirre*, for example, I had at least one more hour of very, very beautiful material that is not in the film now, and also in *Kaspar Hauser*, there were certain scenes that simply deviated too far when seen in the film's full context. During the editing of every film, one has to undergo this kind of cruelty which makes it necessary for you to just tear these scenes from your heart and throw them away and leave them. This is one of the most painful lessons that you have to learn when you make films — that in *each* film there is some sort of a unique inner timing that must be discovered and respected so that this particular subject will *work* for an audience.

And now, as to your question about the difference in the German and the English versions, you should know that only here in the United States have we decided to cut it down by a couple of minutes. I made all these cuts myself, and, although I never thought I would want to do something like this, in making these cuts I have really learned something.

Before making these cuts, we first showed this film in previews, and for these previews we had a very, very average kind of American audience — taxi drivers, for example, and people who just incidentally strolled into the theater — and I found out that *Nosferatu*, in its original cut, in certain moments, all of a sudden, became boring for these audiences. It took a quarter of an hour of strong film after these sequences to pull these audiences back into the film.

So, by making these cuts on *Nosferatu*, I did exactly the same thing that I had already done for *The Great Ecstasy of the Sculptor Steiner*. Basically I made that film for television, but, when it was finished, I ended up with a film that was exactly one hour long. I wanted to have this film televised nationwide in Germany, but the people at the television stations went out of their minds when I came to them with this sixty-minute film, because in Germany we have a very strongly structured pattern for showing things on television. We have — let's say — fifteen minutes of news, no commercials, and then forty-five minutes of documentaries. Forty-five minutes, that's the length of our television documentaries, and so they said to me, "We cannot show this film because it's one hour long, and we would have to change the entire structure of television in order for us to show it!" — this structure is extremely complicated in West Germany because it's state-owned, and the Federation is involved in all of this — and so I said to them, "Let me try to cut it down to forty-five minutes." Then they said, "If you do that, *please* try to make it forty-four minutes and ten seconds long, because we absolutely *need* another fifty seconds for station identification and the introduction for the film." So I went back to the film, and I made it exactly forty-four minutes and ten seconds long. In doing this, I did not feel I had lost a "jewel" out of my crown, because I consider filmmaking as a craft, and I am a craftsman.

In the same way, in regard to *Nosferatu*, I learned that for wider audiences in America the film in its original form would not work properly—so what we are doing now is to release the film in America in the larger cities in the German-language version with English subtitles, and then later we will also show the film in more remote areas in the English version which has been cut by a couple minutes, and this is all right with me. I do not feel hurt about it. Nobody at Fox ever insisted that these cuts be made.

But I must tell you that those preview screenings were such a cruelty! People were asked to fill out and return evaluation cards which asked, "How much did you like the film?" and then you were asked to give the film an "excellent" or "very good" or "good" or "mediocre" or "bad" or "very bad"—and many of these people were so mad at the film that they made a new category on their cards and crossed it, and this category said, "The pits!"
(LAUGHTER FROM AUDIENCE.)

And when you get *that* back, I mean, *hundreds* of those cards . . .
(LAUGHTER FROM AUDIENCE.)

To release a film and to move it out to audiences is *always* a process of extreme cruelty, and one has to learn how to survive it. That's a real art. You have to survive this sort of being kicked in your belly and being kicked in your ass and being slapped in your face—and so, after all, I think that the film is all right like that! People who have seen it with these cuts really don't miss anything.

RE: 20th Century Fox is probably getting all its money back in the French and Italian releases alone.

WH: No, not from the French release, because *Nosferatu* was a coproduction with Gaumont, and Gaumont took all the French territories, and not Fox.

But in France *Nosferatu* was extremely successful. It had an amazing amount of spectators. It's a miracle to me. I don't understand

it. We had eighty-five thousand spectators in the first week in
Paris alone! That's insane for me. It was only outdone by *Star Wars*!
(LAUGHTER FROM AUDIENCE.)

And for Rome I didn't get the exact figures, but Fox told me
that in Italy alone they would get their money back.

All that success in France and Italy gives me a very good feeling
because now we are not under so much pressure to desperately
make every last quick dollar out of this country by pushing it with
an insane sort of campaign. You know this kind of bullshit that
sometimes goes on!

WORKSHOP MEMBER #4: Could I ask you a second question very
briefly? Your films seem to have a great deal of spontaneity, but yet
there's such a very calculated beauty about Schmidt-Reitwein's images. The lighting and even the exact time of day seem to be very
calculated, almost to the degree that is found in Vermeer's paintings.
For example, there's a moment in *La Soufrière* that the camera goes
toward the sun—it's a "lens filter" effect just like the cover of the
current Popol Vuh album—or in *Nosferatu* you have a moment where
the camera goes up to the impending clouds just when the character
played by Bruno Ganz is wondering about his journey. He comes
to the mountain. Then he hears the rumbling, and these clouds are
coming in. All these images seem to be so extremely meticulous, but
yet there remains a definite feeling of spontaneity.

WH: Yes, you are right. Those images are very, very precisely planned.
We had a very clear concept of what we were going to do, and
Schmidt-Reitwein is one of the most excellent cameramen in
the world at organizing light—at knowing exactly how to light a
scene—in order to get these particular effects.

When I first met Schmidt-Reitwein, I saw that he had something very particular about him. He's a man who had spent three
and a half years in prison in Bautzen in East Germany in solitary
confinement. As a result, this man sees certain things that other
people do not see anymore, and so I said to him, "Please come
and live with me," and we lived together for five years in the same
house, and *then* we went to make films together.

For *Nosferatu* we did these scenes so precisely because we knew we were working in a very special field—namely the field of a particular kind of "genre" film which had its own specific rituals and narrative laws and mythic figures that have all been well-known to audiences for at least half a century now. It is just as if, for example, I were going to make a "western," and, by the way, that is *one* thing that I am *not* going to do!

(LAUGHTER FROM AUDIENCE.)

But, if I *were* going to make a "western," however, first I would ask myself, "What is this particular genre about? What are its basic principles? How am I going to modify and develop this genre further?"

And so one of the reasons for this precision in regard to the images is because the genre of vampire films requires extreme stylization, and you have to work very precisely in order to achieve that exact level of stylization.

But it is also true that very much of what you think may be stylization and deliberate construction still may have developed instinctively. It's hard to explain, but, for example, that scene on the mountain with the clouds came about because I simply *liked* those clouds, and I said, "Since we still have film in the camera, let's go ahead and film these clouds." Now, from the viewpoint of narration, it does not make any sense at all to show clouds that barely move for two full minutes, yet in terms of the overall context it's very beautiful and necessary.

On the other hand, some kind of construction is also necessary once in a while. For example, the final shot in *Nosferatu* was filmed on a sandy plain in Holland, and there was a very strong wind so that the sand was blowing at the height of our ankles, and, for this scene, a horse with his black rider is supposed to gallop toward the horizon. In order to obtain the proper effect, I shot, separately from that scene, shots of clouds in single-frame exposure—about one frame every ten seconds—which were then incorporated into the original image, and, when we did this, we turned the shots of the clouds around so that the clouds which you are seeing are actually upside down. It produces a very, very strange effect, and I like it *very* much.

WORKSHOP MEMBER #5: To what degree are your films preconceived, and to what degree are they created as you shoot them?

WH: You should extend your question even further and ask me to what degree are my films developed during editing as well?

But it's not easy to answer your question in a general way because each film somehow has been quite different. But, speaking as generally as possible, I would say that all my screenplays have been written basically as prose-texts. The word "camera" never even appears in any of these texts, and I would say that I've written most of the dialogue for most of the films very often at the very last moment. During the shooting of both *Aguirre* and *Kaspar Hauser*, for example, I didn't even know the dialogue myself ten minutes prior to the shooting, and then, under that enormous pressure of getting everything ready, I absolutely had to produce something, and so I finally wrote the dialogue!

In a similar way, very often I have changed the scripts rather drastically during the shooting and introduced many entirely new scenes into many of the films. In *Stroszek*, for example, the end of the film is now quite different from the way it was originally described in the screenplay. *Aguirre* had a completely different beginning and a completely different ending in the screenplay, and both of these were changed during the shooting. Originally I had wanted to open *Aguirre* with the whole army up on that sixteen-thousandfoot-high glacier. First you would see a thin thread of animals—of pigs, four hundred of them—moving across the glacier. They would be completely dizzy and staggering because of that altitude, and, then, you would see that they were only a very small part of a huge army. Somewhere in between the extremes of that army, there was this smaller army of pigs! But I didn't do it the way I had planned because everyone got sick from the altitude. Two out of three people just couldn't stand it up there, and so I said to myself that I simply could not do it the way it had been planned. I knew that we would have to have a different beginning, and I really like the beginning that *Aguirre* now has very much.

But, as a very rough general rule, I would say about 30 percent of what you see in the final version of my films has not been in the screenplay. Then, during editing, of course, there are a lot of further modifications. More than you would even think possible!

But it is really not very easy to answer your question because every single film that I've made has had a completely different history.

WORKSHOP MEMBER #6: In attempting to get your vision on the screen, in a film like *Aguirre*, for example, just how much *do* you listen to your editor?

WH: My editor, Beate Mainka-Jellinghaus, is very important to me, and I would say that without her I would be only a shadow of myself. But there's always an enormous struggle going on between the two of us, and it's very strange how she behaves during this process. She's *very* rude to me, and she expresses her opinions in a manner that is like the *most* mediocre housewife, but somehow she *always* makes sense. Nevertheless, sometimes she makes mistakes, and we always struggle.

I worked with her for the first time during the editing of *Signs of Life*. I had really made that film with the blood of my heart. I had struggled for it, and, when she saw the material for the first time, it was on a reel that was coiled the wrong way around so that she saw it backwards, and so she would look at the whole reel on the Steenbeck in rapid speed which is five times the normal speed, and she would be seeing it backwards besides, and she would say, "Bullshit!" and throw it all away!

(LAUGHTER FROM AUDIENCE.)

"It's all dreck!" she would say, and I almost fainted when I heard this! After all, here we had worked on this particular sequence for five days, and we thought we had finished with it, and there she was saying, "No!" to all that we had done.

But, eventually, I learned that, just as there are people who have a perfect sense for music and can always identify a certain pitch with mathematical precision, in exactly the same way, she is one of those people who have a perfect sense for *film* material, and I *really* have learned a lot from her! What I have particularly learned from her is that while editing a film you have to become less than a dwarf in front of your own material.

WORKSHOP MEMBER #6: I am still interested in pursuing a little bit further the question of the importance of the editor in your films. In that light I am curious to know whether or not you have ever completed shooting any of your films—your documentaries perhaps even more than your fiction—without having had an editor on the set at any of these times?

WH: With the exception of the time when we filmed *Stroszek*, my editor has never been on the set with us.

WORKSHOP MEMBER #6: Does this mean that most of your films have been shot entirely before your editor has ever even seen the footage?

WH: Yes.

RE: Except that once the editor was almost shot as well!

(LAUGHTER FROM AUDIENCE.)

WH: I think that it has a certain definite value that the editor is *not* on location. It is very important that the editor should keep away from all of our attempts to do things—from all our daily struggles—so that she can form much more of an independent opinion about the material itself.

After I have been filming something, I'm always loaded with certain subjective feelings and certain irrational preferences. For example, it might be that I liked *one* person in a particular film very, very much—someone like Scheitz, for instance—he's mad, but I like him *very* much—and so, when editing *Nosferatu*, in relation to a particular sequence involving Scheitz, Beate Mainka would tell me, "This scene looks good, but in context it doesn't work anymore," and I would see that she was right. Although it would be very hard for me to cut that particular sequence, it would be *correct* to make that cut, and I would do it. But, if she had been with us on location when we shot that sequence with Scheitz—and, by the way, she *also* likes him very much as a person—if she had been on location through all our struggles, she would probably have said, "This scene doesn't work that well in context, but *please* let's leave it in because it's Scheitz!" Do you see my point? I think it is *good* to keep the editor away from where we are filming in order to preserve the *purity* of her opinion.

Having her on location, as we did for *Stroszek*, we discovered had certain definite disadvantages. Afterwards it was *more* difficult for us to edit that film than any of the others.

WORKSHOP MEMBER #6: Yes, I see, but isn't there *any* difference in your approach to the documentaries you've made as opposed to the fictional films? In other words, when you were shooting the documentary on Steiner, for example, once again was the majority of that film shot *before* the editor even had a chance to intervene or offer any suggestions?

WH: Yes, sometimes she wouldn't even know what I was shooting. I would just tell her that I was doing something down in Yugoslavia on a ski jumper, and that would be all. But I would also tell her, "I will finish in mid-March, and so, when I'm finished, let's be ready to start work immediately on the footage."

WORKSHOP MEMBER #6: That's particularly interesting in the light that quite a few Hollywood features are shot in a manner that's just the opposite of your method. In fact, for most of these productions the footage as it comes back in the "dailies" is usually edited that very same day so that they can decide immediately whether or not they want to reshoot anything.

WH: Very often I don't like so much even to see the "dailies" myself, but, even when I do, there are usually only two other people who see them with me. These two people are the cameraman and his assistant. I don't like to have anyone else around.

WORKSHOP MEMBER #7: In the articles and reviews that I've read about your work, I've always wondered why the use of music in your films has been so much neglected by critics in this country.

WH: The music in my films is also very much neglected, if I may interrupt you, in Germany as well. Since *Aguirre*, my friend, Florian Fricke, has done the music for almost all my films—for *Steiner*, for *La Soufrière*, for *Stroszek*, and for *Heart of Glass*—and I've tried to push very hard so that he would be given the National Film Award this year. They've *never* given it to him, and there has been complete neglect of his work. Not even a *single* mention! And this year they just bypassed him once again!

WORKSHOP MEMBER #7: Don't you choose all the music yourself for your films?

WH: Mostly yes, I do it myself.

WORKSHOP MEMBER #7: Do you have any musical training?

WH: No, but I think that there are very few people around who know how to use music properly in films, even those who *do* have formal training. I always keep wondering why it is that the music is so *bad* in most of the films that I see. Of course, there are some very, very good people around like the Taviani brothers. Those bastards are so incredibly lucid in their use of music that they make me feel ashamed. You *have* to see *Padre Padrone*! It is one of the best films I have seen in *ten* years. You must see that film! If it ever plays here in the States, go on the *next* plane to New York or wherever you have to go to be able to see it!

RE: It has already played in Chicago.

WH: You *must* see that film! It's wonderful.

Satyajit Ray, the Bengali filmmaker, also knows how to use music. There's one wonderful film in particular that he has made called *Jalsaghar* (*The Music Room*). Please, if that film *ever* shows somewhere here in the States, try to see that film!

RE: That film has also played here in Chicago. Actually it did pretty well.

WH: But, returning to your question, most of the time I work very, very long on the music. Sometimes it even takes me more time to work on the music than to work on the editing. Almost all of my films are shot in direct sound, but, even so, normally it takes me more time, more energy, more precision in preparing the sound than for working on the camera to establish the shots and the movement of the camera. Just to set up all the reflectors always takes you hours, but to prepare the sound I take even more time! On most occasions it is the sound that decides the outcome of the battle.

I've often seen young filmmakers who, when they finally manage

(35)

to make their first film—when they finally manage to overcome the problems of finances and organization and all the rest—very frequently fail completely with their sound. Very, very often they just do not understand how important sound is, and very, very few people even begin to understand what music *can* be in a film.

Music has always been a matter of major concern for me. Even though I've had no training in music at all, I did all the work on the music for *Even Dwarfs Started Small* by myself. I took a folk song and modified that song by taking out some of the instruments and adding others. Then I found a twelve-year-old girl who could sing that song, and, in order to obtain the right quality in her voice, I went to a cave and recorded her singing.

I've always worked very hard to select the music, but in doing so, I've usually worked very closely with Florian Fricke. For example, to create the music that is used in the opening of *Aguirre* we used a very strange instrument which we called a "choir-organ." This instrument has inside it three dozen tapes running parallel to each other in loops. The first of these tapes has the pitch in fifths, and the next has the whole scale. All these tapes are running at the same time, and there is a keyboard on which you can play them like on an organ so that, when you push one particular key, a certain loop will go on forever and sound just like a human choir but yet, at the same time, very artificial and really quite eerie.

WORKSHOP MEMBER #7: Has any of that music for *Aguirre* been recorded and released commercially?

WH: Yes, there is an album of the music which was released in Europe—in Italy and France, that is, but not in Germany—and I think that it's also being released now here in the United States.

WORKSHOP MEMBER #7: Perhaps you can get it as an import.[7]

WH: Besides the album for *Aguirre*, there's also one for *Heart of Glass*[8] and then, of course, Florian Fricke has made seven or eight albums. Some of these are available now here in this country.[9]

WORKSHOP MEMBER #8: What have been the major influences on your work? Have they come from film? Or from music and the other arts? Or somewhere else?

WH: My strongest influences come from music, but my second strongest influences come from athletics.

Maybe it's hard for you to understand, but in recent years I have become a fanatical listener to very early music. For more than ten years I have been listening more and more to music that goes back beyond the Renaissance, to late medieval music or to music by Schütz[10] or Monteverdi.[11] Orlando di Lasso[12] and Johannes Ciconia[13] are probably names of which you have never even heard, and yet it is their music more than anything else that has influenced my sense of timing and my emotionality.

And athletics is something that I have been involved with *all* my life. I've always been a ski jumper and a soccer player, and yet, when I work on a film, people always seem to think that this kind of work is just the result of some sort of an abstract academic concept of story development or some purely intellectual theory as to how drama should work. They don't seem to realize *all* that is involved in making a film. They don't know, for example, that I'm always afraid of making a film whenever I first start to do it. Right now, my very next project is a film where I truly know that there will be problems that are beyond my personal strength and are beyond my present capacity.

My method of overcoming this kind of fear has always been by working very hard physically on the film. For example, in *Kaspar Hauser*, I worked hard physically in the garden that you see, which was once a potato field, and there I planted all those strawberries and flowers and many other things. Then, even when we were shooting in the interior rooms, I always worked very hard together with the set designer, and together we moved a lot of very heavy furniture. For example, we moved the piano to a certain corner, and then we'd ponder over it, and we'd think, "No, it's not quite right. It shouldn't be there. Somehow the room has no balance." So we would move the piano somewhere else, and then we would move the desk over there where the piano had been, which, in turn, would make it necessary to move the chairs someplace else—and so, simply out of doing this sort of physical work, all of a sudden,

(37)

I began to feel safe, and I was not following just an aesthetic pattern any more. Even though, of course, there was *still* an aesthetic pattern in my film, for me, from then on, the rest of the filming just followed a simple, *physical* pattern.

To give you a specific example of this process, in *Kaspar Hauser*, in order to set up the scene with the deathbed, really all that we had to do was to move the bed to the center of the room and very quickly arrange six or seven people so that they would just be standing or sitting around it, but now, when I see this scene in the film, I realize that it is a *perfectly* balanced image, and yet it only took me five seconds to do it! I just had all these people there, and I said, "You sit here, you stand there, you stand there, you stand there, you sit here," and that was it! It was just a *physical* knowledge which I was able to possess of a certain order that existed within that space, and it is that kind of knowledge which has decided many an important battle for me.

That is precisely the reason why I could not ever make films out of a wheelchair. If I had an accident in a car tomorrow and was paralyzed from my hip downwards and confined to a wheelchair, it would be the immediate end of my filmmaking. I would immediately stop. Even though it would be theoretically possible to continue if there were people to carry me around and help me along, I *still* could not do it anymore.

That's also why I like to carry prints of my films around with me. In 35 mm they each weigh about fifty or sixty pounds. It's awkward to carry them, but I *like* to carry them just in order to have the feeling that I can leave them somewhere in an office or in a projection booth. I can leave them right there on the ground and just walk away. It's just like, when you have had a dream or a nightmare for five nights in a row, then, the very next morning you want to tell your wife immediately what you have been dreaming. You want to communicate this dream immediately to someone, just like this process of giving a *name* to that fear somehow cuts the fear in half, and a film like *Even Dwarfs Started Small* is a perfect example of this process. Just naming the anxiety, just giving a name to a nightmare in order to articulate it, is like taking half the weight off my shoulders. It's *always* a great relief to be able to drop something like that down from off my shoulders, but the embarrassing thing about it is that once I drop one thing, there are already three more sitting on me. I just cannot keep up fast enough, and I don't know what to do about it. I cannot catch up with it anymore. That is why I have tried to work so very fast this last year. I've made two feature films and written two books, and I have two films in preparation, but still it's just not fast enough for me!

RE: I remember you saying that in your next film you were going to employ eleven thousand Peruvian Indians in a project that will involve moving an *actual* steamboat across a mountain from one river system to another. Is that correct?

WH: Yes.

RE: You said that you were not going to use a plastic boat and a Hollywood mountain, but that you were going to use the eleven thousand Indians to move a real iron ship across those mountains! Would you care to elaborate on that?

WH: Yes, but it's a question that's not been completely resolved as yet. In *theory* it would be possible for me to move a ten-thousand-ton steamboat across the highest mountain with just one single finger. If I had the proper system of pulleys powered by a five hundred volt [fold] transmission, then I could easily just pull the rope or simply walk with it for two miles, and the boat would move exactly two inches up the mountain! So, in theory, the problem is easy to resolve. But, in theory, of course, it's even easy to move this earth out of its trajectory! It *can* be done in theory. Archimedes has already stated that, not just me, but so far it's *only* in theory. Yet, in terms of moving the boat across the mountain, I think it *really* can be done. We have some very smart people already working out the solution, but we cannot use modern technology because the story takes place around the turn of the century, and so we will have to use just some pulleys and levers and ropes and other simple things, and somehow we'll do it. You will see. We'll do it!

RE: It's really awesome, like some of the things you accomplished in *Aguirre*.

WH: Yes, but that's kindergarten next to what I am now preparing!

(LAUGHTER FROM AUDIENCE, FOLLOWED BY APPLAUSE.)

For this filming in Peru there is just *so* much preparation! A project like this simply cannot be done unless either you have twenty-five million dollars and a full year's time for the shooting or else you have to take at least three years to prepare it fully so that you will only have to spend about two or three million dollars in order to get it all done. There will be more than ten thousand people in this film, and they *all* have to be organized. They have to have a place to sleep. They have to have costumes. Then we will also need to have two boats that are absolutely identical, and it will take at least half a year just to rebuild a second boat so that it will be an identical twin of the first. All this kind of preparation is very difficult work!

RE: Perhaps you ought to make things a little easier for yourself.

WH: People don't seem to understand that I hate to make difficult films. I hate to have all these problems.

That's the reason I liked making *Woyzeck* so much. I shot that film in just eighteen days, and I edited the film—an entire feature film—completing the final cut in only four days! That's how films *should* be made. That was perfect!

Also one other thing that you should know is that I have been doing more and more writing now. I have learned *how* to write from making films, and I have released five books in the last two and a half years.[14] One day, sooner or later, you will have translations of these books.

But there is *one* text in particular which is closer to my heart than *any* of my films. It is a book that is titled *Of Walking in Ice* which I wrote at nighttime during the shooting of *Nosferatu*. I think that this book will outweigh *all* my films.

RE: I doubt that.

WH: No, you will see.

WORKSHOP MEMBER #9: Would you please tell us something more
about the book you are writing?

WH: I am not writing a book right now, but I have written two prose
books last year. The first one was released in September, and the
second one was released about a month ago. I have also written
three books before these last two, and I've published poetry now
in some magazines.

This book that I mentioned which is the one that I like the
most is basically a diary that I wrote when I walked once from
Munich to Paris. Originally I never thought that I would publish
it because it contained material that was *very* personal. I had never
even read it for the four years since it was written, but, then, during
the shooting of *Nosferatu*, I happened to take it with me—it's a very
tiny little booklet with miniature pencil writing in it—and, all of
a sudden, it struck me that this was not a private text after all. It
was something very much like my films. It had *so* much in it that I
felt that I should try to overcome the embarrassment that would
be involved in making it accessible to other people. So I started to
write it over again. I rewrote the entire diary in order to put it into
a more concise form, leaving out some of those passages that were
still very private, and now I like it very, very much! It's probably
the *best* single work that I've ever done in all my life.

Perhaps that sounds easy to say without my having the proof
here to show you. I hope that it will be translated into English
soon, but it will be *very* difficult to translate because the text lapses
quite often into the Bavarian dialect. There are many expressions
in it that are "wrong"—wrong German in a grammatical sense—
and to discover how to translate this "wrong" German into wrong
English that will still make sense is going to be very difficult. For
example, there's one sentence towards the end of the book that
says in German: "Together we shall cook fire, and we shall stop the
fish." Well, you can *cook* a meal, but you cannot *cook* fire; and you
can *stop* the traffic, but you cannot *stop* the fish. You can *catch* the
fish but not *stop* the fish. This kind of expression sounds "wrong"

(41)

and very, very strange even when you read it in German, but, even so, in German still there is a definite feeling behind these words that somehow they express the absolute truth. Translated into English, however, as literally "together we shall cook fire, and we shall stop the fish," these words lose everything. They *only* sound wrong and nothing more beyond that. This means that there will be a very, very deep problem in translating this book . . . and so I must ask you all to learn German!

(LAUGHTER FROM AUDIENCE.)

WORKSHOP MEMBER #10: I was wondering if you would mind telling us what you feel is the relationship of your work to that of other filmmakers, and if there is anyone in the American cinema today whose work you feel particularly close to?

WH: Yes, there is one filmmaker here in the United States who is very important for me—who is like the Shakespeare of filmmaking—and that is Griffith.[15] So, if you ask me to say who is the *most* important filmmaker here in this country, I would say, "It's Griffith . . . and Griffith . . . and Griffith again!"

Then I also feel very close to the work of some of the Brazilian filmmakers like Ruy Guerra,[16] who appears in *Aguirre* as an actor, and Glauber Rocha.[17]

And, of course, I like some of the Japanese films very much.

There is even some very good filmmaking being done in Germany now, particularly in some of the filmmaking that has a tendency towards the "underground," like the work of Werner Schroeter,[18] for example. It's very strange that a wonderful man like Werner Schroeter is such an unknown here in this country. It is extremely unfortunate that people always focus their attention on just three or four figures and neglect the work of so many others. For instance, I also happen to like *some* of Fassbinder's films.[19] Every fourth film is a good movie!

(LAUGHTER FROM AUDIENCE.)

Yes, and that's what I like about him. He has made some excellent movies, but you should *also* know that we have some very good underground filmmaking as well. I feel very close to these people, particularly Klaus Wyborny,[20] who is a complete unknown even in our own country. Probably you have never even heard of him, but he is a very, very good man.

I also like some of the American underground filmmaking very much, and I even like some of the Hollywood pictures to some extent. You may find it rather strange but I like *very* much *The Broadway Melody of 1940* with Fred Astaire.[21] It's a wonderful movie!

So, you see, there are many, many people around whose work I really like and many films that I see where I have the feeling that I am no longer entirely alone. What I mean to say is that every once in a while it continues to happen to me that when I hear music or see a film just as part of an audience and nothing else, as a part of that audience, it suddenly occurs to me that I am not entirely alone anymore, and that's *exactly* what I try to accomplish with my films. Wherever my films are shown, whatever the size of the audience, if I see people coming out of the screening who give me the feeling that they also have not been alone—that they have had the feeling that they are not entirely alone anymore—then I have done *everything* that I have set out to do! That's *exactly* what I want to do, but much of the time I feel out of tune with most of the industry, with almost everything that's going on—yet, even so, there are *still* enough good people around to make me feel confident.

WORKSHOP MEMBER #10: What is your opinion of film festivals? What good do you think they do?

WH: There are two or three film festivals that I really like. One is Cannes. The second is Telluride, a very small festival in Colorado, and the third is another very small festival that is held in Germany. Everything in between doesn't make much sense.

Cannes is a big circus. It's just like a county fair. Everyone tells me, "Oh, I hate Cannes," and yet they come back every year. Again and again you always see the same people. It really is just a big circus, but, then, it is important to remember that the cinema itself comes from the circus. It has grown out of county fairs, and so I must admit that I like Cannes to some extent even though it's an extremely cruel and crazy place. You can see three hundred films there in two weeks if that is your wish. It's the biggest marketplace for films in the world, and for that reason I like it to some degree.

And I like Telluride in Colorado very much because it is like some sort of a secretive family reunion of very good people, very inspired people, all of them very much alive!

But, in general, I think that there are more film festivals than good films, and, as a result, for these few good films there's always this terrible competition which is always so indecent and so un-dignified. For that reason, I think it would be better if we could somehow cut down the number of festivals to one-third of what we have at present. Then the situation would make much more sense.

But, when I say this, I must also confess that film festivals have been very important as a sort of first taking-off place for me, and so I cannot deny that many festivals still have a certain very real value for many filmmakers. For example, I have always been extremely grateful that my first films were accepted at the New York Film Festival, because that acceptance somehow opened the door a little bit for me in the United States for the very first time.

WORKSHOP MEMBER #11: What do you think has been the political impact of your films?

WH: I doubt the political impact of all films in general to certain de-gree. I think there are *much* stronger means available for making a direct political impact.

For example, a microphone and a man who is an effective public speaker, taken together, are a very real means of influencing politics. It's always the *speakers* who are the greatest politicians. Like Lenin. Or like Adolf Hitler. Even Hitler, when you take a close look at that man, basically he was just a speaker who somehow was able to give expression to the very unclear, strange, aimless fears and desires of the German nation after the Weimar Republic. He was primarily a speaker . . . and so, if you want to go into politics, go get a microphone and become a speaker!

Or another very solid means of making politics is the use of weapons. Go and get a rifle, if you wish. You will quickly discover that a rifle has much more precise effects than *any* film could possibly have!

But, even so, in the long run, I *do* think that films—my films included—could have some sort of political impact eventually because they *might* be able to change our basic perspectives, our basic understanding of things, and changes of this sort, of course, in the long range will have definite effects.

RE: In our discussion tonight, the words "vision" and "visionary" have come up constantly in relation to your work, and what I would like to know now is whether you started to make films and *then* this vision developed from the process of making them, or whether this vision was already there somehow even *before* the films themselves were made?

WH: From the very first, I saw all my films perfectly clearly in my mind, and all my work has just been a series of attempts to make them visible for others. Of course, this process is very difficult. There are always obstacles in making any film. There are always compromises with reality, but sometimes out of these clashes with reality something *new* emerges. I've never ever managed to make a film that is as completely pure as I have seen it originally in my mind. Probably it never can be done in film, and probably that is also one of the reasons why I like the book, *Of Walking in Ice,* so much, because there is no external obstacle to overcome in writing a book like that. Paper is patient, and film is not.

There's really not very much more for me to say at this point because I am *still* searching. But I can assure you that I *do* see something at the horizon, and I am also sure that, to a certain degree, I am already able to articulate what it is that I see. I am still trying to articulate those images that I see at the horizon. I may never be able to succeed completely. Maybe it's absurd and ridiculous even to try—I don't really know—but I *do* know that I won't give up!

(APPLAUSE FROM AUDIENCE.)

RE: Well, thank you very much for being with us this evening.

(APPLAUSE FROM AUDIENCE.)

Notes

1. Walter Steiner, the main protagonist in *The Great Ecstasy of the Sculptor Steiner*.
2. The deaf and blind woman who is the teacher in *Land of Silence and Darkness*.
3. The Facets Multimedia Center.
4. The Chicago International Film Festival.
5. The Film Center of the School of the Art Institute of Chicago.
6. *Bruno der Schwarze* (1970), directed by Lutz Eisholz.
7. For a short time the soundtrack album for *Aguirre* was available as an import (PLD 6040). At the present time, however, the importer has decided to delete from their catalog the majority of their imported "rock" recordings, including several albums by Popol Vuh, and this means that the soundtrack album for *Aguirre* is temporarily unavailable in this country.
8. The soundtrack album by Popol Vuh is currently available in this country as a French import, *Coeur De Verre* (Barclay 900.536), from Jem Records. (As a point of interest, it should be noted that the popular song "Heart of Glass," recorded by Blondie, which, of course, is *not* part of the soundtrack, was, in fact, inspired by the title of Herzog's film. At the time of the recording, however, no one in the group had as yet seen the film.)
9. Other albums by Popol Vuh that have been available in the United States as imports include the following:

Affenstunde (LSB 83460)
The Best of Popol Vuh (PLD 6073)
Brothers of the Shade (Brain 601.167)
Einsjaeger and Siebenjaeger (PLD 6013)
Das Hohelied Salomos (UAS 29781)
Hosianna Mantra (PLD 5094)
In Den Gaerten Pharaos (PLD 6009)
Letzte Tage – Letzte Naechte (UAS 29916)
Seligpreisung (PLD 5082)
Yoga (PLD 6066)

In addition, in the near future Jem Records will become the U.S. distributor for the "import" soundtrack album for Herzog's *Nosferatu*.

10. Heinrich Schütz (1585–1672): Baroque composer, born in Germany, best known for his choral music and as a composer of operas.
11. Claudio Monteverdi (1567–1643): Italian composer whose work bridged the Renaissance and Baroque periods and who is considered to be the founder of modern opera as well as being a renowned madrigalist.
12. Orlando di Lasso (a.k.a. Orlando Lassus or Roland de Lassus) (1532–1594): One of the foremost contrapuntists of the Renaissance, and often considered to be the greatest of the Netherlands composers.
13. Johannes Ciconia (a.k.a. Jean Ciconia de Leodio) (1335–1411): Walloon theorist and composer, born in Liège, died in Italy.

14. The books that Werner Herzog has had published include the following:

Drehbeucher I: Lebenszeichen; *Fata Morgana*; *Auch Zwerge Haben Klein Angefangen* (Munich: Skellig Editions, 1977).

Drehbeucher II: Aguirre, Der Zorn Gottes; *Jeder Fuer Sich Und Gott Gegen Alle*; *Land Des Schweigens Und Der Dunkelheit* (Munich: Skellig Editions, 1977)

Drehbeucher III: Stroszek; *Nosferatu* (Munich: Carl Hanser, 1979)

Greenberg, Alan, *Heart of Glass,* scenario by Herbert Achternbusch and Werner Herzog (Munich: Skellig Editions, 1976)

Vom Gehen im Eis (Munich: Carl Hanser, 1978).

In addition, a "novelization" of Herzog's script for *Nosferatu* has recently been published in the United States:

Monette, Paul, *Nosferatu the Vampyre: A Novel Based on Werner Herzog's Screenplay for the 20th Century Fox Film* (New York: Avon Books, 1979).

15. David Wark Griffith (1875–1948): Preeminent American director whose films include *The Adventures of Dollie* (first film; 1908), *Judith of Bethulia* (1913), *The Birth of a Nation* (1915), *Intolerance* (1916), *Hearts of the World* (1918), *Broken Blossoms* (1919), *Way Down East* (1920), *Orphans of the Storm* (1921), *America* (1924), *Abraham Lincoln* (1930), and *The Struggle* (last "signed" film; 1931).

16. Important contemporary filmmaker born in Mozambique in 1931. He studied in Paris at IDHEC and worked as an assistant director for Jean Delannoy and Georges Rouquier, and made his first feature and most of the films for which he is best known in Brazil. His major films include *Os Cafajestes* (*The Unscrupulous Ones*) (1962), *Os Fuzis* (*The Guns*) (1964), *Sweet Hunters* (1969), and *Os Deuses E Os Mortos* (*The Gods and the Dead*) (1970).

17. Important contemporary filmmaker born in Brazil in 1938. He started to make films in 1958, later worked as a film critic, and became a leading figure in the creation of the Brazilian "Cinema Novo." His major films include *Barravento* (*The Turning Wind*) (1962), *Deus E O Diablo Na Terra Del Sol* (*Black God, White Devil*) (1964), *Terra Em Transe* (*Land in Anguish*) (1967), *Antonio Das Mortes* (1969), *Der Leone Have Sept Cabezas* (*The Lion Has Seven Heads*) (1970), *Cabezas Cortadas* (*Severed Heads*) (1970), and *A Idade Da Terra* (*The Age of the Earth*) (1980). In addition Rocha appeared as an actor in Jean-Luc Godard's *Le Vent D'Est* (*Wind from the East*) (1970).

18. Important contemporary filmmaker born in West Germany in 1945. He was strongly influenced by the European operatic tradition and American underground filmmaking, and started making films in 1968. His major films include *Salome* (1971), *The Death of Maria Malibran* (1972), *Willow Springs* (1973), *Goldflocken* (1976), *Regno Di Napoli* (1978), and *Palermo Oppure* (1980).

19. Rainer Werner Fassbinder: Important contemporary filmmaker born in West Germany in 1946. He was active in Munich theater and "antitheater" prior to his involvement with film, started making films in 1965, and since then has completed more than twenty-five features. His major films include *Liebe Ist Kälter Als*

Der Tod (*Love Is Colder Than Death*) (first feature: 1969), *Warum Läuft Herr R. Amok?* (*Why Does Herr R. Run Amok?*) (1970), *Warnung Vor Einer Heiligen Nutte* (*Beware of a Holy Whore*) (1971), *Händler Der Vier Jahreszeiten* (*The Merchant of Four Seasons*) (1972), *Die Bitteren Tränen Der Petra Von Kant* (*The Bitter Tears of Petra von Kant*) (1972), *Angst Essen Seele Auf* (*Ali: Fear Eats the Soul*) (1974), *Effi Briest* (1974), *Mutter Küsters' Fahrt Zum Himmel* (*Mother Kuster's Trip to Heaven*) (1975), *Faustrecht Der Freiheit* (*Fox and His Friends*) (1975), *Chinesisches Roulette* (*Chinese Roulette*) (1976), and *Despair* (1978). In addition, Fassbinder has appeared as an actor in films by Jean-Marie Straub, Volker Schlöndorff, Ulli Lommel, and many other contemporary German filmmakers.

20. Important contemporary filmmaker born in West Germany in 1945; he started as a student of physics and became involved in the experimental/structuralist mode of filmmaking in the late 1960s. His first films, which were made in the period 1966–1969, were collected into a single multimedia event titled *Daemonische Leinwand* (*Demonic Screen*) that was first exhibited in 1969. His other, more recent films include *Percy McPhee—Agent Des Grauens. Sechste. Siebte. Folge* (*Percy McPhee—Agent of Horror, Chapters Six and Seven*) (1970), *Rot War Das Abenteuer—Blau War Die Reue* (*Red Was the Adventure, Blue Was the Regret*) (1971), *Dallas—Texas & After the Gold Rush* (1971), *The Ideal: Ecstasy and Beauty* (1974), *Fensterfilm* (*Windowfilm*) (1975), *Pictures of a Lost World* (1975), and *Der Ort Der Handlung* (*The Place for Action*) (1977). In addition, Wyborny collaborated with Werner Herzog on the creation of the dream sequences in *Kaspar Hauser: Every Man for Himself and God Against All*.

21. A film directed by Norman Taurog, produced by MGM, in 1940.

(48)

Part 2 Reviews

Aguirre, the Wrath of God

FEBRUARY 9, 1977

Werner Herzog is the most austere of the new German directors, the one most concerned with characters trapped at the extremes of alienation and madness. His films sometimes seem trapped there, too; films like *Fata Morgana*, with its images of desolation in the desert, are so severe and static they're almost painful to watch. But in 1972 he made *Aguirre, the Wrath of God*, about a doomed expedition in South America, and it's one of his most accessible (and horrifying) works.

The Aguirre of the title is a member of Hernando Pizarro's mad 1560 expedition to find El Dorado, the fabled city of gold. In a series of breathtaking opening images, the members of the expedition pick their way down dizzying paths and push through the steaming jungle, dressed with spectacular inappropriateness in medieval armor. They're lost in the trackless wilderness, but their eyes burn with an insane zeal; they're convinced that next day or next week they'll all be as rich as emperors.

Pizarro finally admits defeat and orders Aguirre to lead a search party up the river. He's to report back in a week. If there's no word, Pizarro's group will try to return to their base. Aguirre is played by Klaus Kinski, an actor Herzog has described in an interview as paranoid and schizophrenic ("No one has ever managed to domesticate him"). Whatever his mental state, Kinski invests the film with a frightening intensity. He rules, he kills, he leads, he stares into the camera and we comprehend his secret vision—that he, not Pizarro, will conquer El Dorado and rule an empire.

Herzog, who filmed entirely on location in Peru, shows Aguirre's group on rafts floating down the vast river. The vegetation is so dense that it seems almost impossible to penetrate to the shore. Morale is low, and the heat and fever create a dreamlike, morbid state on the rafts. Aguirre selects the most fatuous member of his group and anoints him "emperor"—possibly because the fact of a ruler will make the nonexistent El Dorado seem more real.

But the overwhelming reality is death. One by one, members of the expedition are picked off by the Indians of the jungle, who are rarely seen but are always there. Poisoned arrows become a fact of life; soldiers drop in the backgrounds of shots concerned with other things. The protected women of the expedition sit by idly, their status sacred, their duty to wait until it is time to populate the new empire.

Herzog finds images to make the river journey an almost physical reality for us. He shows us, for long stretches of film, the muddy torrent of the waters; they never end, and so the expedition will never come to the end of them. He shows us Aguirre's burning eyes, his fiercely set face, his willingness to behead a soldier suspected of disloyalty. And he shows us the attrition of the expedition, as one raft is lost to the Indians and the soldiers on the other are slowly defeated by the arrows, the fever, and their own madness.

The final images are the most bizarre and affecting of all. Everyone has been killed except Aguirre and his sister. She sits quietly in her dress from Spain, patient, unquestioning, possibly insane. Hundreds of little monkeys come aboard the raft and swarm all over it; the meekest citizens of the jungle boldly announcing their victory over the expedition. Aguirre hardly notices them. He stalks back and forth across the deck, now half-awash, vowing that he will personally find El Dorado, will conquer it single-handedly, will populate it by marrying his sister.

Aguirre, the Wrath of God is an obsessive film, about obsession. Because it is more or less based on fact, it's all the more disturbing: here is what greed and madness can bring human beings to. Herzog's other films sometimes speak unclearly; this one speaks in blunt, unforgiving despair.

Nosferatu the Vampyre

OCTOBER 5, 1979

Set aside for the moment the details of the Dracula story. They've lost their meaning. They've been run through a thousand vampire movies too many. It's as easy these days to play Dracula as it is to play Santa Claus. The suit comes with the job. The kids sit on your knee and you ask them what they want and this year they want blood.

Consider instead Count Dracula. He bears a terrible cross, but he lives in a wonderful sphere. He comes backed by music of the masters and dresses in red and black, the colors De Sade found finally the most restful. Dracula's shame as he exchanges intimacies and elegant courtesies with you is that tonight or sometime soon he will need to drink your blood. What an embarrassing thing to know about someone else.

Werner Herzog's *Nosferatu* concerns itself with such knowledge. Nosferatu. A word for the vampire. English permits "vampire movies"—but a "nosferatu movie"? Say "vampire" and your lips must grin. The other word looks like sucking lemons. Perfect. There is nothing pleasant about Herzog's vampire, and this isn't a movie for Creature Feature fans. There are movies for people who like to yuk it up and make barfing sounds, God love 'em, while Christopher Lee lets the blood dribble down his chin, but they're not the audience for *Nosferatu*. This movie isn't even scary. It's so slow it's meditative at times, but it is the most evocative series of images centered around the idea of the vampire that I have ever seen since F. W. Murnau's *Nosferatu*, which was made in 1922.

That is why we're wise to forget the details of the basic Dracula story. *Nosferatu* doesn't pay them heed. It is about the mood and style of vampirism, about the terrible seductive pity of it all. There is a beautiful passage early in the film showing the hero, Jonathan Harker, traveling from his home village to the castle of Dracula. The count has summoned him because he is considering the purchase of another home. Harker makes the journey by horse path. He enters into a high mountain pass filled with tenuous cloud layers that drift by a little too fast, as if God were sucking in his breath. The music is not your standard creepy Looney Tunes, but a fierce melody of exhilaration and dread. Deeper and deeper rides Harker into the cold gray flint of the peaks. Some will say this passage goes on too long and that nothing happens during it. I wish the whole movie were this empty.

Before long, we are regarding the count himself. He is played totally without ego by Klaus Kinski. The count has a monstrous ego, of course—it is Kinski who has none. There is never a moment when we sense this actor enjoying what a fine, juicy, cornpone role he has, with fangs and long sharp fingernails and a cape to swirl. No, Kinski has grown far too old inside to play Dracula like that: he makes his body and gaunt skull transparent, so the role can flicker through.

Sit through *Nosferatu* twice, or three times. Cleanse yourself of the expectation that things will happen. Get with the flow. This movie works like an LP: you can't love the music until you've heard the words so often they're sounds. It's in German with English subtitles. It would be just fine with no subtitles, dubbed into an unknown tongue. The need to know what Dracula is saying at any given moment is a bourgeois affectation. Dracula is always saying, "I am speaking with you now as a meaningless courtesy in preface to the unspeakable event that we both know is going to take place between us sooner rather than later."

Fitzcarraldo

JANUARY 1, 1982

Werner Herzog's *Fitzcarraldo* is a movie in the great tradition of grandiose cinematic visions. Like Coppola's *Apocalypse Now* or Kubrick's *2001: A Space Odyssey*, it is a quest film in which the hero's quest is scarcely madder than the filmmaker's. Movies like this exist on a plane apart from ordinary films. There is a sense in which *Fitzcarraldo* is not altogether successful—it is too long, we could say, or too meandering—but it is still a film that I would not have missed for the world.

The movie is the story of a dreamer named Brian Sweeney Fitzgerald, whose name has been simplified to Fitzcarraldo by the Indians and Spanish who inhabit his godforsaken corner of South America. He loves opera. He spends his days making a little money from an ice factory and his nights dreaming up new schemes. One of them, a plan to build a railroad across the continent, has already failed. Now he is ready with another: he seriously intends to build an opera house in the rainy jungle, twelve hundred miles upstream from the civilized coast, and to bring Enrico Caruso there to sing an opera.

If his plan is mad, his method for carrying it out is madness of another dimension. Looking at the map, he becomes obsessed with the fact that a nearby river system offers access to hundreds of thousands of square miles of potential trading customers—if only a modern steamship could be introduced into that system. There is a point, he notices, where the other river is separated only by a thin finger of land from a river that is already navigated by boats. His inspiration: drag a steamship across land to the other river, float it, set up a thriving trade, and use the profits to build the opera house—and then bring in Caruso! This scheme is so unlikely that perhaps we should not be surprised that Herzog's story is based on the case of a real Irish entrepreneur who tried to do exactly that.

The historical Irishman was at least wise enough to disassemble his boat before carting it across land. In Herzog's movie, however, Fitzcarraldo determines to drag the boat up one hill and down the other side in one piece. He enlists engineers to devise a system of blocks and pulleys that will do the trick, and he hires the local Indians to work the levers with their own muscle power. And it is here that we arrive at the thing about *Fitzcarraldo* that transcends all understanding: Werner Herzog determined to literally drag a real steamship up a real hill, using real tackle and hiring the local Indians! To produce the movie, he decided to do personally what even the original Fitzgerald never attempted.

Herzog finally settled on the right actor to play Fitzcarraldo, author of this plan: Klaus Kinski, the shock-haired German who starred in Herzog's *Aguirre, the Wrath of God* and *Nosferatu*, is back again to mastermind the effort. Kinski is perfectly cast. Herzog's original choice for the role was Jason Robards, who is also gifted at conveying a consuming passion, but Kinski, wild-eyed and ferocious, consumes the screen. There are other characters important to the story, especially Claudia Cardinale as the madam who loves Fitzcarraldo and helps finance his attempt, but without Kinski at the core it's doubtful this story would work.

The story of Herzog's own production is itself well-known and has been told in Les Blank's *Burden of Dreams*, a brilliant documentary about the filming. It's possible that every moment of *Fitzcarraldo* is colored by our knowledge that Herzog was "really" doing the things we see Fitzcarraldo do. (The movie uses no special effects, no models, no opticals, no miniatures.) Perhaps we're even tempted to give the movie extra points because of Herzog's ordeal in the jungle.

But *Fitzcarraldo* is not all sweat and madness. It contains great poetic images of the sort Herzog is famous for: an old phonograph playing a Caruso record on the deck of a boat spinning out of control into a rapids, Fitzcarraldo frantically oaring a little rowboat down a jungle river to be in time to hear an opera, and of course the immensely impressive sight of that actual steamship resting halfway up a hillside.

Fitzcarraldo is not a perfect movie, and it never comes together into a unified statement. It is meandering, and it is slow and formless at times. Perhaps the conception was just too large for Herzog to shape. The movie does not approach perfection as *Aguirre* did. But as a document of a quest and a dream, and as a record of man's audacity and foolish, visionary heroism, there has never been another movie like it.

(57)

Burden of Dreams

DIRECTED BY LES BLANK

JANUARY 1, 1982

Les Blank's *Burden of Dreams* is one of the most remarkable documentaries ever made about the making of a movie. There are at least two reasons for that. One is that the movie being made, Werner Herzog's *Fitzcarraldo*, involved some of the most torturous and dangerous on-location shooting experiences in film history. The other is that the documentary is by Les Blank, himself a brilliant filmmaker, who is unafraid to ask difficult questions and portray Herzog, warts and all.

The story of Herzog's *Fitzcarraldo* is already the stuff of movie legend. The movie was shot on location deep within the rain forests of South America, one thousand miles from civilization. When the first version of the film was half-finished, its star, Jason Robards, was rushed back to New York with amoebic dysentery and forbidden by his doctors to return to the location. Herzog replaced Robards with Klaus Kinski (star of his *Aguirre, the Wrath of God*), but meanwhile costar Mick Jagger left the production because of a commitment to a concert tour. Then the Kinski version of *Fitzcarraldo* was caught in the middle of a border war between tribes of Indians. The whole production was moved twelve hundred miles, to a new location where the mishaps included plane crashes, disease, and attacks by unfriendly Indians. And all of those hardships were on top of the incredible task Herzog set himself to film: he wanted to show his obsessed hero using teams of Indians to pull an entire steamship up a hillside using only block and tackle!

Blank and his associate Maureen Gosling visited both locations of Herzog's film. Their documentary includes the only available record of some of the earlier scenes with Robards and Jagger. It also includes scenes in which Herzog seems to be going slowly mad, blaming the evil of the jungle and the depth of his own compulsions. In *Fitzcarraldo*, you can see the incredible strain as men try to pull a steamship up a sharp incline, using only muscle power and a few elementary principles of mechanics. In *Burden of Dreams*, Blank's camera moves back one more step, to show the actual mechanisms by which Herzog hoped to move his ship. A giant bulldozer is used to augment the block-and-pulley system, but it proves barely equal to the task, and at one point the Brazilian engineer in charge of the project walks off, warning that lives will be lost.

What drives Herzog to make films that test his sanity and risk his life and those of his associates? Stanley Kauffmann, in the *New Republic*, argued that, for Herzog, the purpose of film is to risk death, and each of his films is in some way a challenge hurled at the odds. Herzog has made films on the slopes of active volcanoes, has filmed in the jungle and in the middle of the Sahara, and has made films about characters who live at the edges of human achievement. *Burden of Dreams* gives us an extraordinary portrait of Herzog trapped in the middle of one of his wildest dreams.

Where the Green Ants Dream

JANUARY I, 1984

Werner Herzog believes in the voodoo of locations, in the possibility that if he shoots a movie in the right place and at the right time, the reality of the location itself will seep into the film and make it more real. He has filmed on the slopes of active volcanoes and a thousand miles up the Amazon, and in his new movie, *Where the Green Ants Dream*, he goes to a godforsaken, heat-baked stretch of Australian outback. This is grim territory, but it is sacred land to the Aborigines, who believe that this is the place where the green ants go to dream and that if their dreams are disturbed, unspeakable calamities will rain down on future generations. The Aborigines' belief is not shared by a giant mining company, which wants to tear open the soil and search for uranium.

As the movie opens, the company is in the process of setting off explosions, so geologists can listen to the echoes and choose likely mining sites. The Aborigines sit passively in the way of the explosions, refusing to move, insisting that the ants must not be awakened. We meet the characters on both sides: the tall, gangly mining engineer; the implacable tribal leaders; the supercilious president of the mining company; and the assorted eccentrics who have washed up on this desert shore.

Herzog has said that he thinks in images, not ideas, and that if he can find the correct pictures for a film, he's not concerned about its message. In *Where the Green Ants Dream*, his images include an old woman sitting patiently in the outback, an opened can of dog food on the ground in front of her, waiting for a pet dog that has been lost in a mine shaft. Then we see a group of Aborigines sitting in the aisle of a supermarket on the exact spot where the last tree in the district once stood; it was the tree under which the men of the tribe once stood to "dream" their children before conceiving them. We also see an extraordinary landscape, almost lunar in its barren loneliness.

We do not see any ants, but then perhaps that is part of Herzog's plan. One of the strangest things about this film (strange if you are not familiar with Herzog, who is the strangest of all living directors) is that nothing in this movie is based on anthropological fact. The beliefs, customs, and behavior of the Aborigines, for example, are not inspired by research into their actual lives but are a fiction, made up by Herzog for his screenplay. The confrontation between the mining company and the Aborigines is likewise not based on yesterday's headlines but is symbolic, representing for Herzog similar "real" stories but in a more dramatic form. Even the details about the life cycles of the ants are made up; Herzog has no idea if there are really ants in the outback.

But there is a reality, nevertheless, in this odd film, and it comes out of the two conflicting sets of beliefs. The Aborigines sit and wait, inspired by deep currents of faith and tradition, and the engineers are always in motion, convinced that success lies in industry and activity. The conflict is everywhere in the world today, and Herzog didn't need to make it up, only to find the pictures for it.

Little Dieter Needs to Fly

OCTOBER 2, 1998

"Men are often haunted," Werner Herzog tells us at the beginning of *Little Dieter Needs to Fly*. "They seem to be normal, but they are not." His documentary tells the story of such a haunted man, whose memories include being hung upside down with an ant nest over his head and fighting a snake for a dead rat they both wanted to eat.

The man's name is Dieter Dengler. He was born in the Black Forest of Germany. As a child, he watched his village be destroyed by American warplanes, and one flew so close to his attic window that for a split second he made eye contact with the pilot flashing past. At that moment, Dieter Dengler knew that he needed to fly.

Dengler is now in his fifties, a businessman living in Northern California. He invites us into his home, carefully opening and closing every door over and over again, to be sure he is not locked in. He shows us the stores of rice, flour, and honey under his floor. He obsesses about being locked in, about having nothing to eat. He tells us his story.

As an eighteen-year-old, he came penniless to America. He enlisted in the Navy to learn to fly. He flew missions over Vietnam, but "that there were people down there who suffered, who died—only became clear to me after I was their prisoner." He was shot down, made a prisoner, became one of only seven men to escape from prison camps and survive. He endured tortures by his captors and from nature: dysentery, insect bites, starvation, hallucinations.

Werner Herzog's *Little Dieter Needs to Fly* lets Dieter tell his own story, which he does in rushed but vivid English, as if fearful there will not be time enough if he doesn't speak fast. As he talks, Herzog puts him in locations: his American home, his German village of Wildberg, and then the same Laotian jungles where he was shot down. Here certain memories are reenacted: he is handcuffed by villagers, is made to march through the forest, and demonstrates how he was staked down at night. "You can't imagine what I'm thinking," he says.

The thing about storytelling is that it creates pictures in our heads. I can "see" what happened to Dieter Dengler as clearly as if it has all been dramatized, and his poetry adds to the images. "As I followed the river, there was this beautiful bear following me," he remembers. "This bear meant death to me. It's really ironic—the only friend I had at the end was death." At another point, standing in front of a giant tank of jellyfish, he says, "This is basically what Death looks like to me," and Herzog's camera moves in on the dreamy floating shapes as we hear the sad theme from *Tristan and Isolde*. Now here is an interesting aspect. Dieter Dengler is a real man who really underwent all of those experiences (and won the Medal of Honor, the DFC, and the Navy Cross because of them). His story is true. But not all of his words are his own. Herzog freely reveals in conversation that he suggested certain images to Dengler. The image of the jellyfish, for example—"that was my idea," Herzog told me. Likewise the opening and shutting of the doors, although not the image of the bear.

Herzog has had two careers, as the director of some of the strangest and most fascinating features of the last thirty years, and of some of the best documentaries. Many of his docs are about obsessed men: the ski jumper Steiner, for example, who flew so high he overjumped his landing areas. Or Herzog himself, venturing onto a volcanic island to interview the one man who would not leave when he was told the volcano would explode.

Herzog sees his mission as a filmmaker is not to turn himself into a recording machine but to be a collaborator. He does not simply stand and watch, but arranges and adjusts and subtly enhances so that the film takes the materials of Dengler's adventure and fashions it into a new thing.

(63)

You meet a person who has an amazing story to tell, and you rarely have the time to hear it or the attention to appreciate it. The attendants in nursing homes sit glued to their Stephen King paperbacks; the old people around them have stories a thousand times scarier to tell. A colorful character dies and the obituaries say countless great stories were told about him—but at the end, did anybody still care to listen? Herzog starts with a balding middle-aged man driving down a country lane in a convertible and listens, questions, and shapes, until the life experience of Dieter Dengler becomes unforgettable. What an astonishing man! we think. But if we were to sit next to him on a plane, we might tell him we had seen his movie, and make a polite comment about it, and go back to our magazine. It takes art to transform someone else's experience into our own.

My Best Fiend

FEBRUARY 11, 2000

Werner Herzog made five films starring Klaus Kinski. No other director ever worked with him more than once. Midway in their first
film, *Aguirre, the Wrath of God* (1972), Kinski threatened to walk off
the set, deep in the Amazon rain forest, and Herzog said he would
shoot him dead if he did. Kinski claims in his autobiography that he
had the gun, not Herzog.

Herzog says that's a lie. Kinski describes Herzog in the book as a
"nasty, sadistic, treacherous, cowardly creep." Herzog says in the film
that Kinski knew his autobiography would not sell unless he said
shocking things — so Herzog helped him look up vile words he could
use in describing the director.

And so it goes on, almost a decade after Kinski's death, the unend-
ing love-hate relationship between the visionary German filmmaker
and his muse and nemesis in five films. Herzog's new documentary
My Best Fiend traces their history together. They had one of the most
fruitful and troubled relationships of any director-actor team.

Together they made *Aguirre*, about a mad conquistador in the
Peruvian jungle; *Fitzcarraldo*, about a man who used block and tackle
to pull a steamship from one Amazonian river system to another;
Nosferatu (1979), inspired by Murnau's silent vampire classic; *Woyzeck*
(1979), about a nineteenth-century army private who seems mad to
others because he sees the world in his own alternative way; and *Cobra
Verde* (1987), about a slave trader in Africa. All of their collaborations

contain extraordinary images, but the sight of Kinski running wild inside an army of naked, spear-carrying amazons in *Cobra Verde* may be the strangest.

Reviewing *Woyzeck*, I wrote: "It is almost impossible to imagine Kinski without Herzog; reflect that this 'unforgettable' actor made more than 170 films for other directors—and we can hardly remember a one." Consider, too, that their strange bond began long before Herzog stood behind a camera.

Herzog told me how they had met. When he was twelve, he said, "I was playing in the courtyard of the building where we lived in Munich, and I looked up and saw this man striding past, and I knew at that moment that my destiny was to direct films, and that he would be the actor." Kinski was known for his scorn of both films and acting, and claimed to choose projects entirely on the basis of how comfortable he would be on the location. Yet when Herzog summoned him to the rain forest for *Aguirre*, where he would have to march through the jungle wearing Spanish armor and end up on a sinking raft with gibbering monkeys, he accepted. Why? I asked him once, and he replied grimly: "It was my fate." Herzog believes in shooting on location, arguing that specific places have a voodoo that penetrates the film. *Fitzcarraldo* could have been shot in comfort, not nine hundred miles up the Amazon, with special effects and a model boat—but Herzog insisted on isolating his crew and in hauling a real boat up a real hill. When engineers warned him the ropes would snap and cut everyone in two, he dismissed the engineers. That's all the more intriguing when you learn that Kinski was even more hated than Herzog on the location.

In *My Best Fiend*, Herzog recalls that local Indians came to him with an offer to kill Kinski. "I needed Kinski for a few more shots, so I turned them down," he says. "I have always regretted that I lost that opportunity." He learned early about Kinski's towering rages. The actor actually lived for several months in the same flat with Herzog's family and once locked himself in the bathroom for two days, screaming all the while and reducing the porcelain fixtures "to grains the size of sand." Only once, on *Aguirre*, was he able to fully contain his anger in his character—perhaps because Aguirre was as mad as Kinski—and there he gave one of the great performances in the cinema. Herzog revisits the original locations, recalling fights they had and showing the specific scenes that were shot just afterward.

There must have been good times, too, although Herzog only shows one of them—a happy day at the Telluride Film Festival. *My Best Fiend* suffers a little by not having footage to cover more of Herzog's sharpest memories (Les Blank's legendary documentary *Burden of Dreams*, shot on location during *Fitzcarraldo*, shows the two men at each other's throats).

But as a meditation by a director on an actor, it is unique; most showbiz docs involve the ritual exchange of compliments. *My Best Fiend* is about two men who both wanted to be dominant, who both had all the answers, who were inseparably bound together in love and hate, and who created extraordinary work—while all the time each resented the other's contribution.

(67)

Invincible

OCTOBER 4, 2002

Werner Herzog's *Invincible* tells the astonishing story of a Jewish strongman in Nazi Germany, a man who in his simple goodness believes he
can be the "new Samson" and protect his people. He is a blacksmith in
Poland in 1932 when discovered by a talent scout, and soon becomes
the headliner in the Palace of the Occult, in Berlin, which is run by
the sinister Hanussen (Tim Roth), a man who dreams of becoming
Minister of the Occult in a Nazi government.

The strongman, named Zishe Breitbart, is played by a Finnish ath-
lete named Jouko Ahola, twice winner of the title World's Strongest
Man. Much of the movie's uncanny appeal comes from the contrast
between Ahola's performance, which is entirely without guile, and
Roth's performance, which drips with mannered malevolence. Standing between them is the young woman Marta (Anna Gourari), who is
under Hanussen's psychological power, and whom the strongman loves.

Invincible is based, Herzog says, on the true story of Breitbart,
whose great strength contradicted the Nazi myth of Aryan superior-
ity. I can imagine a dozen ways in which this story could be told badly,
but Herzog has fashioned it into a film of uncommon fascination in
which we often have no idea at all what could possibly happen next.
There are countless movies about preludes to the Holocaust, but I
can't think of one this innocent, direct and unblinking. In the face of
gathering evil, Zishe trusts in human nature, is proud of his heritage,
and believes strength and goodness (which he confuses) will triumph.

The movie has the power of a great silent film, unafraid of grand gestures and moral absolutes. Its casting of the major characters is crucial and instinctively correct. Tim Roth is a sinister charlatan, posing as a man with real psychic powers, using trickery and showmanship as he jockeys for position within the emerging Nazi majority. There is a scene where he hypnotizes Marta, and as he stares boldly into the camera I wondered, for a moment, if it was possible to hypnotize a movie audience that way. Late in the film there is a scene where his secrets are revealed, and he makes a speech of chilling, absolute cynicism. Another actor in another movie might have simply gnashed his teeth, but Roth and Herzog take the revelations as an opportunity to show us the self-hatred beneath the deception.

As for Jouko Ahola, this untrained actor, who seems by nature to be good-hearted and uncomplicated, may never act again, but he has found the one perfect role, as Maria Falconetti did in *The Passion of Joan of Arc*. He embodies the simple strongman. The camera can look as closely as it wants and never find anything false. A naive man from a backward town, not especially devout, he gets into a fight when Polish customers in a restaurant insult him and his little brother as Jews. A little later, entering a circus contest, he watches as the strongman lifts a boulder—and then puts an end to the contest by lifting the strongman and the boulder.

The talent scout takes him to see his first movie. Soon he is in Berlin, where Hanussen sizes him up and says, "We will Aryanize you. A Jew should never be as strong as you." Zishe is outfitted with a blond wig and a Nordic helmet, and presented as "Siegfried." He becomes a great favor of Nazi brownshirts in the audience, as Hanussen prattles about "the strength of the body against the dark powers of the occult." But Zishe's mind works away at the situation until finally he has his solution, tears off the helmet and wig, and identities himself as a Jew.

Here as throughout the film Herzog avoids the obvious next scene. Is Hanussen outraged? To a degree. But then he reports: "There's a line three blocks long outside! It's the Jews. They all want to see the new Samson." And then, at a time when Hitler was on the rise but the full measure of Jewish persecution was not yet in view, the Palace of the Occult turns into a dangerous pit where audience members are potentially at one another's throats.

This is the first feature in ten years from Herzog, one of the great visionaries among directors. He strains to break the bonds of film structure in order to surprise us in unexpected ways. His best films unashamedly yearn to lift us into the mythical and the mystical. "Our civilization is starving for new images," he once told me, and in *Invincible* there is an image of a bleak, rocky seashore where the sharp stones are littered with thousands or millions of bright red crabs, all mindlessly scrabbling away on their crabby missions. I think this scene may represent the emerging Nazi hordes, but of course there can be no literal translation. Perhaps Herzog wants to illustrate the implacable Darwinian struggle from which man can rise with good heart and purpose.

The strongman in *Invincible* is lovable, and so deeply moving, precisely because he is not a cog in a plot, has no plan, is involved in no machinations, but is simply proud of his parents, proud to be a Jew, in love with the girl, and convinced that God has made him strong for a reason. He may be wrong in his optimism, but his greatest strength is that he will never understand that. The Roth character is equally single-minded, but without hope or purpose — a conniver and a manipulator.

Watching *Invincible* was a singular experience for me, because it reminded me of the fundamental power that the cinema had for us when we were children. The film exercises the power that fable has for the believing. Herzog has gotten outside the constraints and conventions of ordinary narrative, and addresses us where our credulity keeps its secrets.

Grizzly Man

AUGUST 12, 2005

If I show weakness, I'm dead. They will take me out, they will decapitate me, they will chop me up into bits and pieces—I'm dead. So far, I persevere. I persevere. So speaks Timothy Treadwell, balanced somewhere between the grandiose and the manic, in Werner Herzog's *Grizzly Man.*

He is talking about the wild bears he came to know and love during thirteen summers spent living among them in Alaska's Katmai National Park and Reserve. In the early autumn of 2003, one of the bears took him out, decapitated him, chopped him up into bits and pieces, and he was dead. The bear also killed his girlfriend.

In happier times, we see Treadwell as a guest on the David Letterman show. "Is it going to happen," Letterman asks him, "that we read a news item one day that you have been eaten by one of these bears?" Audience laughter. Later in the film, we listen to the helicopter pilot who retrieved Treadwell's bones a few days after he died: "He was treating them like people in bear costumes. He got what he deserved. The tragedy of it is, he took the girl with him."

Grizzly Man is unlike any nature documentary I've seen; it doesn't approve of Treadwell, and it isn't sentimental about animals. It was assembled by Herzog, the great German director, from some ninety hours of video that Treadwell shot in the wild, and from interviews with those who knew him, including Jewel Palovak of Grizzly People, the organization Treadwell founded. She knew him as well as anybody.

Treadwell was a tanned, good-looking man in his forties with a

Prince Valiant haircut who could charm people and, for thirteen years, could charm bears. He was more complex than he seemed. In rambling, confessional speeches recorded while he was alone in the wilderness, he talks of being a recovering alcoholic, of his love for the bears and his fierce determination to "protect" them—although others point out that the bears were safe enough in a national park, and he was doing them no favor by making them familiar with humans. He had other peculiarities, including a fake Australian accent to go with his story that he was from Down Under and not from New York.

"I have seen this madness on a movie set before," says Herzog, who narrates his film. "I have seen human ecstasies and darkest human turmoil." Indeed, madness has been the subject of many of his films, fact and fiction, and watching Treadwell I was reminded of the ski jumper Steiner in another Herzog doc, the man who could fly so far that he threatened to overshoot the landing area and crash in the parking lot. Or the hero of *Fitzcarraldo*, obsessed with hauling a ship across land from one river to another.

"My life is on the precipice of death," Treadwell tells the camera. Yet he sentimentalizes the bears and is moved to ecstasy by a large steaming pile of "Wendy's poop," which is still warm, he exults, and was "inside of her" just minutes earlier. He names all the bears, and provides a play-by-play commentary as two of the big males fight for the right to court "Satin."

During his last two or three years in the wilderness, Treadwell was joined by his new girlfriend, Amie Huguenard. Herzog is able to find only one photograph of her, and when she appears in Treadwell's footage (rarely) her face is hard to see. Treadwell liked to give the impression that he was alone with his bears, but Herzog shows one shot that is obviously handheld—by Amie, presumably.

Ironically, Treadwell and Huguenard had left for home in the September when they died. Treadwell got into an argument with an Air Alaska employee, canceled his plans to fly home, returned to the "Grizzly Maze" area where most of the bears he knew were already hibernating, and was killed and eaten by an unfamiliar bear that, it appears, he photographed a few hours before his death.

The cap was on his video camera during the attack, but audio was recorded. Herzog listens to the tape in the presence of Palovak and then tells her: "You must never listen to this. You should not keep it. You should destroy it because it will be like the white elephant in your room all your life." His decision not to play the audio in his film is a wise one, not only out of respect to the survivors of the victims, but because to watch him listening to it is, oddly, more effective than actually hearing it. We would hear, he tells us, Treadwell screaming for Amie to run for her life, and we would hear the sounds of her trying to fight off the bear by banging it with a frying pan.

The documentary is an uncommon meeting between Treadwell's loony idealism and Herzog's bleak worldview. Treadwell's footage is sometimes miraculous, as when we see his close bond with a fox who has been like his pet dog for ten years. Or when he grows angry with God because a drought has dried up the salmon run and his bears are starving. He *demands* that God make it rain and, what do you know, it does.

Against this is Herzog, on the soundtrack: "I believe the common character of the universe is not harmony, but hostility, chaos, and murder." And over footage of one of Treadwell's beloved bears: "This blank stare" shows not the wisdom Treadwell read into it, but "only the half-bored interest in food."

"I will protect these bears with my last breath," Treadwell says. After he and Amie become the first and only people to be killed by bears in the park, the bear that is guilty is shot dead. His watch, still ticking, is found on his severed arm. I have a certain admiration for his courage, recklessness, idealism, whatever you want to call it, but here is a man who managed to get himself and his girlfriend eaten, and you know what? He deserves Werner Herzog.

The White Diamond

SEPTEMBER 2, 2005

Werner Herzog's documentary *The White Diamond* is not about a diamond but about an airship, one of the smallest ever built, designed to float above the canopy of equatorial rain forests. Every niche in the jungle is exploited by plants, animals, and insects that have evolved to make a living there, and biologists believe that undiscovered species might live their entire lives 80 or 120 feet from the ground.

Herzog introduces us to a London researcher named Graham Dorrington, who dreams of reaching out from his airship to study specimens on the ceiling of the jungle. Like many of Herzog's subjects, he is a dreamer who talks a little too fast and smiles when he doesn't seem to be happy: when a sudden storm threatens to tear his airship to pieces, he says he is philosophical, and we see that he isn't.

Dorrington's airship is shaped like an upside-down teardrop with a tail. It carries a two-man gondola and is powered and steered by small motors. It uses helium gas, which will not burn, unlike hydrogen gas, which caught fire inside the Hindenburg and brought an end to an era when the giant zeppelins served tourist routes connecting Europe, Brazil, India, and the United States. The zeppelins were cigar-shaped ships that were hard to turn, Dorrington says, unlike his ship, which can pivot in the air. That is the theory, anyway, as he explains his motors and his switches, and we hear the voice of Herzog, always filled with apprehension, telling us, "He did not know then that this particular switch would cause a huge problem later."

Dorrington tested an earlier airship in 1993 in Sumatra, and that ended with catastrophe, Herzog tells us. Dorrington describes the death of his cinematographer, Dieter Plage, who fell from a gondola after it was broken on the high branches of a tree by a sudden wind. "It was an accident," Dorrington says, and all agree, but he blames himself every day. Now he is ready to try again.

His airship was built in a huge hangar outside London that once housed dirigibles. Strange, that it cannot be tested there, but must be transported to South America and the rain forests of Guyana. Dorrington is a man after Herzog's heart—Herzog, the director who could have filmed *Aguirre, the Wrath of God* and *Fitzcarraldo* a few miles from cities, and insisted on filming them hundreds of miles inside the rain forest. Herzog has made a specialty of finding obsessives and eccentrics who push themselves to extremes; see his current doc, *Grizzly Man*, about Timothy Treadwell, who lived among the bears of Alaska until one killed him.

Now watch what happens during the first test flight. Herzog has an argument with Dorrington. The scientist wants to fly solo. Herzog calls it "stupid" that the first flight might take place without a camera on board. (It might, of course, be the only flight.) Herzog has brought along two cinematographers, but insists he must personally take the camera up on the maiden voyage. "I cannot ask a cinematographer to get in an airship before I test it myself," he says. As Herzog buckles himself into the gondola, we reflect that if Dorrington's standards were those that Herzog insists on, *Dorrington* would not allow *Herzog* to get in the airship until he had tested it himself. It is sublimely Herzogian that this paradox is right there in full view.

There are some dicey moments when the ship goes backward when it should go forward, and Herzog observes a motor burning out and pieces of a propeller whizzing past his head. The flight instructor who pilots the expedition's ultralight aircraft says Dorrington has not practiced "good airmanship." Dorrington moans that "seven different systems" failed. We wonder if the catastrophe in Sumatra will be repeated.

There is breathtaking footage of the ship's flights, as it skims the forest canopy, and descends to dip a toe in the river. Mournful, vaguely ecclesiastical music accompanies these images. The vast Kaieteur Falls fascinates the party; its waters are golden-brown as they roar into a maelstrom, and countless swifts and other birds fly into a cave behind the curtain of water. Mark Anthony Yhap, a local man employed by the expedition, relates legends about the cave. The team doctor, Michael Wilk, has himself lowered on a rope with a video camera to look into the cave. It is typical of a Herzog project that the doctor would be "an experienced mountain climber." It is sublimely typical of Herzog that he does *not* show us the doctor's footage of the cave, after Yhap argues that its sacred secret must be preserved. What is in the cave? A lot of guano, is my guess.

There are times when this expedition causes us to speculate that the Monty Python troupe might have based its material on close observation of actual living Britons. Consider the "experiment" to determine if the downdraft of the waterfall is so strong it would threaten the airship. Dorrington and Herzog tie together four brightly colored birthday balloons and hang a glass of champagne from them as ballast. Sure enough, the balloons are sucked into the mist.

Mark Anthony Yhap is one of the film's riches. Known as "Redbeard," he is a Rastafarian who gives the film its title, saying the airship looks like a "big white diamond floating around in the sunrise." Yhap is fond of his red rooster, a mighty bird that has five wives who present him with five eggs every morning. Toward the end of the film Yhap is given his own chance to ride in the airship and enjoys it immensely, but regrets that he could not take along his rooster.

Although *The White Diamond* is entire of itself, it earns its place among the other treasures and curiosities in Herzog's work. Here is one of the most inquisitive filmmakers alive, a man who will go to incredible lengths to film people living at the extremes. In *La Soufrière*, a 1977 documentary released on DVD last month, he journeys to an island evacuated because of an impending volcanic eruption, to ask the only man who stayed behind why he did not leave. What he is really asking, what he is always asking, is why he had to go there to ask the question.

Rescue Dawn

JULY 13, 2007

When he was a child during World War II, Dieter Dengler had an attic
room on a German hillside overlooking a valley. One day an American
fighter plane roared past "only feet away," he recalled. The plane's
canopy was down; he made eye contact with the pilot for a moment
and instantly knew that he wanted to fly.

Werner Herzog's *Rescue Dawn*, based on Dengler's experiences,
begins early in the Vietnam War, when Dengler is a US Navy pilot
stationed on a carrier in the Gulf of Tonkin. At eighteen, he enlisted
to get American citizenship and to fly. Assigned to a secret, illegal
bombing mission over Laos, he is shot down, and the film involves his
experiences as a prisoner of war, his escape, and his harrowing fight for
survival in the jungle. He was one of only seven Americans to escape
from a Vietcong POW camp and live. Dengler (played by Christian
Bale) scoffs at his flimsy bamboo "cell" until a fellow American tells
him, "Don't you get it? It's the jungle that is the prison."

His ordeal includes tortures in the camp (he is hung by his heels
with an ants' nest fastened to his head) and an agonizing trek through
the jungle, at first with a fellow American named Duane (Steve Zahn),
then alone. Herzog makes no attempt to pump this story up into a
thrilling adventure. There is nothing thrilling about dysentery, starvation, insect bites, and despair. The film heads instead into the trem-
bling fear at Dengler's center.

This feature has been long on the mind of Herzog, who film for film is the most original and challenging of directors. He used the real Dieter Dengler in a 1997 documentary named *Little Dieter Needs to Fly*, in which he took Dengler back to the jungle, and together they re-created his escape while Dengler provided a breathlessly intense narration.

Considering that Herzog made both films, it is perhaps not surprising that the "fictional" feature is more realistic than the documentary. With Herzog there is always free trade between fact and fantasy. *Little Dieter* shows Dengler obsessively opening and closing the doors and windows of his house, to be sure he is not locked in. Not true, Herzog told me; the director added that detail for dramatic effect. Also in the doc, Dengler imagines himself being followed through the jungle by a bear, who came to represent "death, my only friend." That seems to be a fantasy, yet Herzog says it was real. But there is no bear in *Rescue Dawn*. Too hard to believe, is my guess.

The movie is, indeed, perhaps the most believable that Herzog has made. For a director who gravitates toward the extremes of human behavior, this film involves extreme behavior, yes, but behavior forced by the circumstances. There is nothing in it we cannot, or do not, believe. I was almost prepared to compare it to the classic storytelling of John Huston when I realized it had crucial Herzogian differences.

One is the use of location. Asked long ago why he went to so much trouble to shoot *Aguirre, the Wrath of God* and *Fitzcarraldo* hundreds of miles into the rain forests of the Amazon, he said it involved "the voodoo of location." He felt actors, directors, cinematographers, and perhaps the film itself absorbed something from where the shooting took place. Even for his vampire film *Nosferatu* (1979), he sought out the same locations F. W. Murnau used in the silent 1922 original.

In *Rescue Dawn*, filmed in the jungles of Thailand, there is never the slightest doubt we are in the jungle. No movie stars creeping behind potted shrubbery on a back lot. The screen always looks wet and green, and the actors push through the choking vegetation with difficulty. We can almost smell the rot and humidity. To discuss the power of the performances by Bale, Zahn, and Jeremy Davies (as another POW) would miss the point unless we speculated about how much of the conviction in their work came from the fact that they were really doing it in the hellish place where it was really done.

The other Herzog touch is the music. Herzog recoils from conventional scores that mirror the action. Here he uses not upbeat adventure music, but brooding, introspective, doomy music by Klaus Badelt; classical and chamber performances; and passages by Popol Vuh, the German New Age band that supplied so much of the feeling in *Aguirre* (1972) and *Fitzcarraldo* (1982).

Rescue Dawn opened in some US markets on July Fourth. It is about a man who won the Purple Heart, the Air Medal, the Distinguished Flying Cross, and the Navy Cross (none of which the movie mentions). Given the times we live in, is it an upbeat, patriotic film? Not by intention. It is simply the story of this man. When he is finally greeted back aboard his aircraft carrier, there is no "mission accomplished" banner, and when he is asked for his words of advice for the cheering crew, he says: "Empty that which is full. Fill that which is empty. If it itches, scratch it."

Walking to Werner

DIRECTED BY LINAS PHILLIPS

AUGUST 10, 2007

The free spirit Werner Herzog, whose *Rescue Dawn* is now a considerable success, likes to walk. He has inspired at least two would-be filmmakers to follow in his footsteps. Faithful readers will know that I value Herzog's films beyond all measure and never tire of telling the famous story of the time he learned his dear friend, the film historian Lotte Eisner, was dying in Paris. Thereupon he set off to walk from Munich to Paris, convinced she would not die before his arrival, and he was quite right.

Another time, he walked completely around Albania ("because at that time, you could not enter Albania"). When I invited him to my film festival a few years ago, he was lowered from a plateau in a South American rain forest, made his way by log canoe and trading skiff to a pontoon plane that took him to a boat, etc. "He came because it was so difficult," his wife, Lena, told me. "If Werner had been in Los Angeles, it would have been too easy, and he might not have made the journey."

His friend, the director Dusan Makavejev, notes in his new book *Cinema of the Balkans* that Werner once came looking for an ancestor in Croatia and followed his footsteps up a Serbian mountain, hoping to help end the war raging around him. "The essential things in life," Herzog has said, "I would cover on foot, regardless of the distance."

Herzog, his films, and his walking inspired the filmmaker Linas Phillips to make *Walking to Werner*, the story of his walking 1,200 miles from Seattle to Los Angeles to meet the great man. Currently in post-production is another film, by Herzog admirer Lee Kazimir of Chicago, who walked from Madrid to Kiev. In a message to me, Kazimir quoted Herzog: "If you want to make films, you should skip film school. Instead, you should make a journey of 5,000 kilometers alone, on foot. While walking, you would learn more about what cinema truly means than you would in five years of sitting in classrooms."

Herzog doesn't encourage these journeys when he is the destination. He warned Phillips that he would not be at home when the young man arrived, because he would be in Laos, Burma, and Thailand filming *Rescue Dawn*. Phillips persisted. Kazimir wrote asking his blessing, and Herzog told me: "I had instant hesitations, and told him so, as he was going to make his voyage a public event. Traveling on foot was in my understanding a thing you had to do as a man exposing yourself in the most direct way to life, to *pura vida,* and this should stay with oneself." Kazimir also persisted.

Walking to Werner is the first of these films to open, but it doesn't steal the thunder of the second, because both will be about the trekkers and not Herzog. The real interest in the film is not the journey or even Linas Phillips (who comes across a little like Timothy Treadwell of Herzog's *Grizzly Man*), but the people he meets on the way.

Some of them look like you might want to cross the road to avoid them, but with one hostile exception and one sad exception, they are all sane, friendly, cheerful, and encouraging. I was particularly moved by Robert, a laid-off Boeing worker in Seattle, who sees Phillips in a bar and tells him, "Don't end up like me." Phillips asks him to voice the title of the movie for him and requests his blessing at the start of the walk.

Another man, Eli, was walking without food because "he no longer saw the worth of life and was too cowardly to kill himself." Phillips, who discovers "when you travel on foot, there's no small talk," meets another man, who tells him, "I have no soul." Five miles down the road, the man catches up with Phillips and corrects himself: "I do have a soul."

These encounters are supplemented by Phillips's narration, and by the voice of Herzog, often taken from Les Blank's amazing documentary

Burden of Dreams, the record of Herzog filming *Fitzcarraldo*. That was the film in which Herzog, shunning special effects, hauled a real steamboat over a real hill between two river systems. "Moviegoers have to be able to trust their eyes," he explained.

With his long blond hair flowing from beneath his Tilley hat (the hiker's friend), Phillips is once mistaken for a woman and firmly corrects the impression. His face turns red and weathered, his toes develop blisters, and although he often stays in motels, he has a disconcerting tendency to walk late into the night and in the rain. He looks exhausted much of the time; did he train for this walk? As gigantic trucks roar past, he calculates the odds of one of them killing him.

One reason for his long hair may be that, in 2003, he performed a one-man show, *Linus as Kinski*, in New York. Having embodied the look and spirit of Klaus Kinski, the temperamental subject of Herzog's doc *My Best Fiend*, Phillips still seems to be in costume.

He communicates with Herzog by e-mail. "If you want to walk, do it for some other reason," the director advises him. When Phillips speculates about going on to Thailand to film a meeting to end his film, Herzog replies, "An interview would be a cheap end to your film."

Encounters at the End of the World

JULY 10, 2008

Read the title of *Encounters at the End of the World* carefully, for it has two meanings. As he journeys to the South Pole, which is as far as you can get from everywhere, Werner Herzog also journeys to the prospect of man's oblivion. Far under the eternal ice, he visits a curious tunnel whose walls have been decorated by various mementos, including a frozen fish that is far away from its home waters. What might travelers from another planet think of these souvenirs, he wonders, if they visit long after all other signs of our civilization have vanished?

Herzog has come to live for a while at the McMurdo Research Station, the largest habitation on Antarctica. He was attracted by underwater films taken by his friend Henry Kaiser, which show scientists exploring the ocean floor. They open a hole in the ice with a blasting device, then plunge in, collecting specimens, taking films, nosing around. They investigate an undersea world of horrifying carnage, inhabited by creatures so ferocious, we are relieved they are too small to be seen. And also by enormous seals who sing to one another. In order not to limit their range, Herzog observes, the divers do not use a tether line, so they must trust themselves to find the hole in the ice again. I am afraid to even think about that.

Herzog is a romantic wanderer, drawn to the extremes. He makes as many documentaries as fiction films, is prolific in the chronicles of his curiosity and here moseys about McMurdo, chatting with people who have chosen to live here in eternal day or night.

They are a strange population. One woman likes to have herself zipped into luggage and performs this feat on the station's talent night. One man was once a banker and now drives an enormous bus. A pipefitter matches the fingers of his hands together to show that the second and third are the same length—genetic evidence, he says, that he is descended from Aztec kings.

But I make the movie sound like a travelogue or an exhibit of eccentrics, and it is a poem of oddness and beauty. Herzog is like no other filmmaker, and to return to him is to be welcomed into a world vastly larger and more peculiar than the one around us. The underwater photography alone would make a film, but there is so much more. Consider the men who study the active volcanoes of Antarctica, and sometimes descend into volcanic fumes that open to the surface, although they must take care, Herzog observes in his wondering, precise narration, not to be doing so when the volcano erupts. It happens that there is another movie opening today in Chicago that also has volcanic tubes (*Journey to the Center of the Earth*). Do not confuse the two. These men play with real volcanoes.

They also lead lives revolving around monster movies on video, and a treasured ice cream machine and a string band concert from the top of a Quonset hut during the eternal day. And they have modern conveniences of which Herzog despairs, like an ATM machine, in a place where the machine, the money inside it, and the people who use it must all be airlifted in. Herzog loves these people, it is clear, because like himself they have gone to such lengths to escape the mundane and test the limits of the extraordinary. But there is a difference between them and Timothy Treadwell, the hero of *Grizzly Man*, Herzog's documentary about a man who thought he could live with bears and not be eaten, and was mistaken. The difference is that Treadwell was a foolish romantic, and these men and women are in this godforsaken place to extend their knowledge of the planet and of the mysteries of life and death itself.

Herzog's method makes the movie seem like it is happening by chance, although chance has nothing to do with it. He narrates as if we're watching movies of his last vacation—informal, conversational, engaging. He talks about people he met, sights he saw, thoughts he had. And then a larger picture grows inexorably into view. McMurdo is perched on the frontier of the coming suicide of the planet. Mankind has grown too fast, spent too freely, consumed too much, and the ice cap is melting, and we shall all perish. Herzog doesn't use such language, of course; he is too subtle and visionary. He is nudged toward his conclusions by what he sees. In a sense, his film journeys through time as well as space, and we see what little we may end up leaving behind us. Nor is he depressed by this prospect, but only philosophical. We came, we saw, we conquered, and we left behind a frozen fish.

His visit to Antarctica was not intended, he warns us at the outset, to take footage of "fluffy penguins." But there are some penguins in the film, and one of them embarks on a journey that haunts my memory to this moment, long after it must have ended.

Note: Herzog dedicated this film to me. I am deeply moved and honored.

Bad Lieutenant: Port of Call, New Orleans

NOVEMBER 18, 2009

Werner Herzog's *Bad Lieutenant: Port of Call, New Orleans* creates a dire portrait of a rapist, murderer, drug addict, corrupt cop, and degenerate paranoid who's very apprehensive about iguanas. It places him in a devastated New Orleans not long after Hurricane Katrina. It makes no attempt to show that city of legends in a flattering light. And it gradually reveals itself as a sly comedy about a snaky but courageous man.

No one is better at this kind of performance than Nicolas Cage. He's a fearless actor. He doesn't care if you think he goes over the top. If a film calls for it, he will crawl to the top hand over hand with bleeding fingernails. Regard him in films so various as *Wild at Heart* and *Leaving Las Vegas*. He and Herzog were born to work together. They are both made restless by caution.

In the gallery of bad cops, Terence McDonagh belongs in the first room. Everyone will think of Harvey Keitel's lieutenant in Abel Ferrara's masterpiece *Bad Lieutenant* (1992) for the obvious reason. I hope this film inspires you to seek out that one. It deserves to be sought. Ferrara is Shakespearean in his tragedy, Herzog more like Cormac McCarthy. Sometimes on the road to hell you can't help but laugh.

In a city deserted by many of its citizens and much of its good fortune, McDonagh roams the midnight streets without supervision. He serves and protects himself. He is the Law, and the Law exists for his personal benefit. Lurking in his prowler outside a nightclub, he sees a young couple emerge and follows them to an empty parking lot. He stops them, searches them, finds negligible drugs on the man, begins the process of arrest. The man pleads. He's afraid his father will find out. He offers a bribe. McDonagh isn't interested in money. He wants the drugs and the girl, whom he rapes, excited that her boyfriend is watching.

The film's only similarities with the Ferrara film are in the title and the presentation of a wholly immoral drug addict. It's not what a movie is about but how it's about it. Ferrara regards his lieutenant without mercy. Herzog can be as forgiving as God. An addict in need can be capable of about anything. He will betray family, loved ones, duty, himself. He's driven. Because addiction is an illness (although there is debate), we mustn't be too quick to judge. Drugs and alcohol are both terrible, but drugs can drive a victim more urgently to ruin. (87)

Herzog shows McDonagh lopsided from back pain. He begins with prescription Vicodin and moves quickly to cocaine. As a cop, he develops sources. He steals from other addicts and from dealers. In the confusion after Katrina, he steals from a police evidence room. George Carlin said, "What does cocaine feel like? It makes you feel like some more cocaine."

McDonagh has a girlfriend named Frankie (Eva Mendes). She's a hooker. He's OK with this. He gives her drugs, she sometimes has them for him. They share something an addict craves: sympathy and understanding. They stand together against the horrors. He's also close to his sixtyish father, Pat (Tom Bower), not close to Pat's fortyish partner Genevieve (Jennifer Coolidge). His father has a history with AA. Genevieve is a bosomy all-day beer drinker. They live in a slowly decaying rural manse somewhere in the parish. Pat knows what to look for in his son and sees it.

Colorful characters enrich McDonagh's tunnel-visioned life. There's hip-hop star Alvin "Xzibit" Joiner as Big Fate, a kingpin who holds the key to the execution of five Nigerian drug dealers. Fairuza Balk as a cop and McDonagh's sometime lover. Brad Dourif as his bookie (he gambles, too). Val Kilmer as his partner, in an uncharacteristically laid-back performance. Maybe we couldn't take Cage and Kilmer both cranked up to eleven. Bower plays McDonagh's father as a troubled man but one with good instincts. Coolidge, with great screen presence as always, changes gears and plays a MI-wouldn't-LF.

The details of the crime need not concern us. Just admire the feel of the film. Peter Zeitlinger's cinematography creates a New Orleans unleavened by the picturesque. Herzog as always pokes around for the odd detail. Everyone is talking about the shots of the iguanas and the alligator, staring with cold reptilian eyes. Who else but Herzog would *hold* on their gaze? Who else would foreground them, placing the action in the background? Who but Cage could regard an iguana sideways in a look of suspicion and disquiet? You need to keep an eye on an iguana. The bastards are always up to something.

Bad Lieutenant: Port of Call, New Orleans is not about plot, but about seasoning. Like New Orleans cuisine, it finds that you can put almost anything in a pot if you add the right spices and peppers and simmer it long enough.

Yet surely *Bad Lieutenant: Port of Call, New Orleans* is an odd title? Let me give you my fantasy about that. Herzog agrees with Ed Pressman to do a remake of the 1992 film, which Pressman also produced. Pressman is no fool and knows a Werner Herzog remake will be nothing like the original. Abel Ferrara is outraged, as well he might be; Martin Scorsese picked *Bad Lieutenant* as one of the ten best films of the 1990s.

"Gee, I dunno," Pressman says. "Maybe we *should* change the title. How about talking a line from the screenplay? How about calling it 'Port of Call, New Orleans'?"

"We will compromise," Herzog says with that Germanic precision he uses when explaining something he needs to make clear. "We will call it 'Bad Lieutenant: Port of Call, New Orleans.'" He's not going to back down from Ferrara. These are proud men.

Note: Brothers Alan and Gabe Polsky also produced this film along with Ed Pressman. Alan says that no one wanted to make a remake of Ferrara's movie, least of all Herzog, but they did want to continue the arc of the character from the previous film, sort of like an anthology. So a new script was developed and they used the "Bad Lieutenant" nomenclature as Pressman wanted. However, Herzog added "port of call, New Orleans" to make it clear that it wasn't a remake.

My Son, My Son, What Have Ye Done

APRIL 7, 2010

Werner Herzog's *My Son, My Son, What Have Ye Done* is a splendid example of a movie not on autopilot. I bore my readers by complaining about how bored I am by formula movies that recycle the same moronic elements. Now here is a film where Udo Kier's eyeglasses are snatched from his pocket by an ostrich, has them yanked from the ostrich's throat by a farmhand, gets them back all covered with ostrich mucus, and tells the ostrich, "Don't you do that again!"

Meanwhile, there is talk about how the racist ostrich farmer once raised a chicken as big as, I think, forty ordinary birds. What did he do with it? "Ate it. Sooner pluck one than forty." Knowing as I do that Herzog hates chickens with a passion beyond all reason, I flashed back to an earlier scene in which the film's protagonist talks with his scrawny pet flamingoes. Is a theme emerging here? And the flamingo who regards the camera with a dubious look, is it doing an imitation of the staring iguana in Herzog's *Bad Lieutenant*?

For me it hardly matters if a Herzog film provides conventional movie pleasures. Many of them do. *Bad Lieutenant*, for example. *My Son, My Son, What Have Ye Done*, on the other hand, confounds all convention and denies all expected pleasures, providing instead the delight of watching Herzog feed the police hostage formula into the Mixmaster of his imagination. It's as if he began with the outline of a stunningly routine police procedural and said to hell with it, I'm going to hang my whimsy on this clothesline.

He casts Willem Dafoe as his hero, a homicide detective named Hank Havenhurst. Dafoe is known for his willingness to embrace projects by directors who work on the edge. He is an excellent actor and splendid here at creating a cop who conducts his job with tunnel vision and few expected human emotions. It is difficult to conceive of a police officer showing less response to a madman ostrich farmer.

His case involves a man named Brad McCullum, played by the inspired Michael Shannon as a man with an alarming stare beneath a lowering brow. He kills his mother with a wicked antique sword, as she sits having coffee with two neighbors. He likes to repeat "Razzle Dazzle," which reminded me of "Helter Skelter," and yes, the movie is "inspired by a true story." His mother (Grace Zabriskie) is a woman who is so nice she could, possibly, inspire murder, especially in a son who has undergone life-altering experiences in the Peruvian rain forest, as this one has—and why, you ask? For the excellent reason, I suspect, that Herzog could go through great difficulty to revisit the Urubamba River in Peru, where he shot part of *Fitzcarraldo* (1982). Perhaps whenever he encounters an actor with alarming eyes, like Klaus Kinski or Shannon, he thinks, "I will put him to the test of the Urubamba River!"

Detective Havenhurst takes over a command center in front of the house where Brad is said to be holding two hostages (never seen) and interviews Brad's fiancée Ingrid (Chloë Sevigny) and his theater director, Lee Meyers (Udo Kier). Both tell him stories that inspire flashbacks. Indeed, most of the film involves flashbacks leading up to the moment when Brad slashed his mother. Ingrid is played by Sevigny as a dim, sweet young woman lacking all insight and instinct for self-protection, and Meyers is played by Kier as a man who is incredibly patient with Brad during rehearsals for the Greek tragedy *Elektra*. That's the one where the son slays his mother.

The memories of Lee Meyers inspire the field trip to the ostrich farm run by Uncle Ted (Brad Dourif). If you've been keeping track, the film's cast includes almost *only* cult actors often involved with cult directors: Dafoe, Shannon, Sevigny, Kier, Dourif, Zabriskie, and I haven't even mentioned Cannes prize winner Irma P. Hall and Gabriel

Pimentel. Havenhurst's partner is played by Michael Pena, who is not a cult actor but plays one in this movie. Little jest. For that matter, the film's producer is David Lynch, one of the few producers who might think it made perfect sense that a cop drama set in San Diego would require location filming on the Urubamba River.

There is a scene in this movie that involves men who appear to be yurt dwellers from Mongolia, one with spectacular eyebrow hairs. I confess I may have had a momentary attention lapse, but I can't remember what they had to do with the plot. Still, I'll not soon forget those eyebrows, which is more than I can say for most scenes at the 60 percent mark in most cop movies. I am also grateful for two very long shots, one involving Grace Zabriskie and the other Gabriel Pimentel, in which they look at the camera for thirty or forty seconds while flanked with Shannon and another one of the actors. These look like freeze frames, but you can see the actors moving just a little. What do these shots represent? Why, the director's impatience with convention, that's what.

(91)

I have now performed an excellent job of describing the movie. Can you sense why I enjoyed it? It you don't like it, you won't be able to claim I misled you. I rode on an ostrich once. Halfway between Oudtshoorn and the Cango Caves, it was.

Cave of Forgotten Dreams

APRIL 27, 2011

In 1994, French archaeologists, searching for air plumes that might reveal the presence of a cave, found it again. They had to descend a narrow opening to its floor, far below on the original entrance level. It is their entry route that Werner Herzog follows in his spellbinding film, *Cave of Forgotten Dreams*.

Herzog filmed in 3-D, to better convey how the paintings follow and exploit the natural contours of the ancient walls. The process also helps him suggest how the humans of the upper Paleolithic Era might have seen the paintings themselves, in the flickering light of their torches.

Access to Chauvet Cave, named for one of its discoverers, was immediately closed off by the French government, and a locked steel door now bars the way to the air shaft. Behind that door, the cave's guardians enforce a strict regime. Herzog is allowed a four-man crew, including himself. They are limited to four cold-panel lights, powered from battery belts. They dare step only on two-foot-wide aluminum pathways that have been installed. They are allowed four hours each day. If anyone has to leave for any reason—even to get a screwdriver—that day's visit is over; the guardians want to shield the cave's air supply.

Surely men must have been painting somewhere before these cave walls were covered. It is hard to believe that these confident lines and shapes came into being without prelude. Or was there something innate in these forms? Accurate carbon dating suggests that other artists returned to the cave at least two thousand years after the first ones arrived and continued the work in the same style.

Only two very small sculptures in the cave show human forms. One is a woman, with her sexual organs exaggerated to dramatize her fertility. The paintings themselves are all of animals, an astonishing variety, providing a bestiary of the valley at the time: mammoths, cave bears, lions, bison, panthers, horses, rhinos. The rhinos have what are surely exaggerated horns, suggesting a desire to emphasize their power. Some of the drawings repeat horns and legs in an obvious attempt to depict movement.

In addition to the footprint, there are poignant signs that humans were here. Near the original entrance, where outside light was still present, many visitors left their palm prints on a wall in red ochre. Were these the artists' marks? Calling cards? Why did many leave them? A palm print stands out: one man had a damaged little finger. Further back in the cave, they found another mark with the same finger. His two visits and a child's footprint remain after thirty millennia.

The restriction of four small portable light panels works to Herzog's advantage; as they move, they suggest how the flickering torches might have created an illusion of movement in those repeated features. The space was so limited it was impossible for his crew to stay out of many shots, and their shadows dance on the walls, just as the shadows of forgotten ancestors must have danced in the torchlight. Herzog's inspiration is to show us the paintings as the cave's original visitors must have seen them. I have seen perfectly lighted photographs of other cave paintings that are not so evocative.

Herzog says that in general, he dislikes 3-D. But he believes there are occasions when 3-D is appropriate, and this film is one of them. I saw it with bright, well-focused digital projection. Apart from a one-shot joke at the very end, he never allows his images to violate the theater space; he uses 3-D as a way for us to enter the film's space, instead of a way for it to enter ours. He was correct to realize how useful it would be in photographing these walls. To the degree that it's possible for us to walk behind Herzog into that cave, we do so.

Into the Abyss

NOVEMBER 9, 2011

Into the Abyss may be the saddest film Werner Herzog has ever made. It regards a group of miserable lives, and in finding a few faint glimmers of hope it only underlines the sadness.

The documentary centers on two young men in prison. Michael Perry is on death row in Huntsville, Texas, America's most productive assembly line for executions, and on the day Herzog spoke with him he had eight days to live. Jason Burkett, his accomplice in the stupid murders of three people, is serving a forty-year sentence. They killed because they wanted to drive a friend's red Camaro.

Herzog opposes the death penalty, which America and Japan are the only developed nations still imposing. But the film isn't a polemic. Herzog became curious about the case, took a small crew to Huntsville and Conroe, Texas, where the murders took place, and spoke to the killers, members of their families, and those of their victims. He obtains interviews of startling honesty and impact. I've learned that he met his subjects only once, on the day of the interviews, and the film presents their first conversations. I've long felt Herzog's personality is compelling and penetrating, and in evidence I could offer this film about Texans who are so different from the German director.

Herzog keeps a much lower profile than in many of his documentaries. He is not seen, and his off-camera voice quietly asks questions that are factual, understated and simply curious. His subjects talk willingly. He asks difficult follow-up questions. He is very interested not in the facts (there is no doubt about guilt here), but in looking into the eyes and souls of people who were directly involved.

Why did Perry die and not Burkett, when both were convicted for the same crimes? We meet Burkett's father, Delbert, who also is in prison serving a life sentence. In his testimony at his son's trial, he blamed himself for the boy's worthless upbringing. This apparently influenced two women jurors to pity the boy—or perhaps identify with the father. Delbert seems today a decent and reflective man. He bitterly regrets that he failed to take advantage of a college scholarship, dropped out of high school not long before graduation, and went wrong. He sees his mistake clearly now—too late for himself, too late for his son.

Perry and Burkett are uneducated, rootless, callow, lacking in personal resources. Delbert perhaps has benefitted from life in prison, as his son may. We meet Melyssa Burkett, who married Jason Burkett in prison and is now pregnant with his child—although, as Herzog observes, conjugal visits were not allowed. How did she become pregnant? She did, that's all. Herzog never sensationalizes, never underlines, expresses no opinions. He listens. (95)

We also meet Captain Fred Allen, who was for many years in charge of the guard detail on Huntsville's death row, including the years in which George Bush turned down one appeal after another. He starts talking with Herzog and is swept up by memory and emotion, explaining why one day he simply walked away from his job and decided, after overseeing more than one hundred executions, that he was opposed to the death penalty. What he has to say about one crucial event in his life is one of the most profound statements I can imagine about the death penalty.

The people in this film, without exception, cite God as a force in their lives. The killers, their relatives, the relatives of their victims, the police, everyone. God has a plan. It is all God's will. God will forgive. Their lives are in His hands. They must accept the will of the Lord. Condemned or bereft, guilty or heartbroken, they all apparently find comfort in God's plan. What Herzog concludes about their faith he does not say.

Opposition to the death penalty, in part, comes down to this: no one deserves to be assigned the task of executing another person. I think that's what Captain Allen is saying. Herzog may agree, although he doesn't say so. In some of his films he freely shares his philosophy and insights. In this film, he simply looks. He always seems to know where to look.

Part 3   Interviews

At Cannes Film Festival

CANNES, FRANCE—On the day after *Fitzcarraldo* had its world premiere at the Cannes Film Festival, I sat and had tea with Werner Herzog, the West German who directed it. Werner Herzog is a strange, deep, visionary man. With other directors, I have an interview. With Herzog, I have an audience.

He does not speak of small matters. He would not say so, but he obviously sees himself as one of the most important artists of his time—and so, to tell the truth, do I. He makes films that exist outside the usual categories. He takes enormous risks to make them. In a widely discussed article in the *New Republic*, Stanley Kauffmann wondered if it is an item of Herzog's faith that he must risk his life with every movie he makes.

It is a logical question. Herzog makes movies about people who have larger dreams and take greater risks than ordinary men. Herzog does the same. He once went with a small crew to an island where a volcano was about to explode. He wanted to interview a man who had decided to stay behind and die. Herzog has also made movies in the middle of the Sahara, and twice he has risked his life and the lives of his associates on risky film projects in the Amazon rain jungles.

His *Aguirre, the Wrath of God* (1972) told the story of one of Pizarro's mad followers who pressed on relentlessly into the jungle in a doomed quest for El Dorado. Now there is *Fitzcarraldo*, based on the true story of an Irishman who tried to haul a whole steamship over dry land from one Amazonian river system to another.

As nearly everybody must know by now, Werner Herzog did the same thing in filming *Fitzcarraldo*. But Herzog's historical inspiration (who was named Fitzgerald) had the good sense to disassemble *his* steamship before hauling it overland; Herzog used winches and pulleys to haul an entire boat overland *intact*. And that afternoon over tea at Cannes, he was not modest about his fear: "*Apocalypse Now* was only a kindergarten compared to what we went through," he said.

At forty, he is a thin, strongly built man of average height, with hair swept back from a broad forehead. He usually wears a neat mustache. He spent an undergraduate year at a university in Pennsylvania and speaks excellent English; he once made a movie, *Stroszek*, on location in northern Wisconsin, and it included a striking image of the lost American Dream, as his hero, Bruno, looked in despair as the bank repossessed his mobile home and left him contemplating the frozen prairie.

I had seen *Fitzcarraldo* the day before. I also had seen Les Blank's *Burden of Dreams*, an unblinking, unsentimental documentary about the making of *Fitzcarraldo*. It is good to see the two films together, because Blank's documentary paints a portrait of Herzog seemingly going mad under the strain of making his impossible movie. I asked Herzog about that: did he really crack up during his months in the rain jungle and his legendary problems with civil wars, disease, Indian attacks, and defecting cast and crew members?

"Sanity?" he said. "For that you don't have to fear. I am quite sane." He somehow sounded like the vampire hero of his *Nosferatu*. He sipped tea. "I make sense. I don't push myself to the edge." Having said that, he proceeded to contradict it: "It is only the project that counts. If the nature of the project makes it necessary for me to go very far, I would go anywhere. How much you have to suffer, how little sleep you get . . . I am the last one to look for a situation like that, but the last one to back out if it's necessary."

He looked over the veranda of the hotel, at the palm trees in the spring sunshine.

"I would go down in hell and wrestle a film away from the devil if it was necessary," said the man who had just told me he didn't push himself to the edge.

Do you feel you have a personal mission to fulfill? I asked. Other directors sign up Goldie Hawn and shoot in Los Angeles. You sign up Klaus Kinski and disappear into the rain forest.

"If you say 'mission,' it sounds a little heavy," he said. "I would say 'duty' or 'purpose.' When I start a new film, I am a good soldier. I do not complain. I will hold the outpost even if it is already given up. Of course I want to win the battle. I see each film more like a high duty that I have."

Is your duty to the film, I asked, or does the film itself fulfill a duty to mankind? Even as I asked the question, I realized that it sounded grandiose, but Herzog nodded solemnly. He said his duty was to help mankind find new images, and, indeed, in his films there are many great and vivid images: a man standing on a drifting raft, surrounded by gibbering monkeys; a ski jumper so good that he overjumps a landing area; men deaf and blind from birth, feeling the mystery of a tree; a man asleep on the side of a volcano; midgets chasing runaway automobiles; a man standing on an outcropping rock in the middle of a barren sea; a man hauling a ship up the side of a mountain.

"We do not have adequate images for our kind of civilization," Herzog said. "What are we to look at? The ads at the travel agent's of the Grand Canyon? We are surrounded by images that are worn out, and I believe that unless we discover new images, we will die out. Die like the dinosaurs. And I mean it physically."

He leaned forward, speaking intensely, as if time were running out. "Frogs do not apparently need images, and cows do not need them, either. But we do. Michelangelo in the Sistine Chapel for the first time articulated human pathos in a new way that was adequate to the understanding of his time. I am not looking to make films in which actors stand around and say words that some screenwriter has thought were clever. That is why I use midgets, and a man who spent twenty-four years in prisons and asylums (Bruno S., the hero of *Stroszek*) and the deaf and blind, and why I shoot with actors who are under hypnosis, for example. I am trying to make something that has not been made before."

I said *Fitzcarraldo* almost seemed to be about itself: a film about a man who hauled a ship up a hill, made by a man who hauled a real ship up a real hill to make a film.

"It was not planned like that," Herzog said. "It was not planned to be as difficult as it was. It came to a point where the purpose of the film, the making of the film, the goals of the film and how to make the film all became one and the same thing: to get that ship up the hill. When Jason Robards fell ill and returned to America, before I replaced him with Klaus Kinski, I thought about playing Fitzcarraldo myself. I came very close."

Why did you have to use a real boat?

"There was never any question in my mind about that. All those trashy special effects and miniatures that you see in Hollywood movies have caused audiences to lose trust in their eyes. Here, in my film, they are given back trust in their own eyes. When the boat goes up the mountain, people look at the screen, looking for something to tell them it's a trick, but it's no trick. Instinctively, they sense it. An image like that gives you courage for your own dreams."

He smiled, a little grimly. "It's a film," he said, "that will not have a remake. That man who is going to make this film again has to be born first." He paused for thought. "The mad King Ludwig II of Bavaria," he said, "could have made this film."

I observed that in *Burden of Dreams* there seemed to be some controversy over the safety and practicality of hauling the ship up the hill.

"I had engineers," Herzog said, "and I disposed of them. I had the basic idea of winches and pulleys, of a chain of combined winches. In prehistory, you can see that perhaps man did the same thing. In Brittany, there are huge boulders of rock that may have been moved two miles up ramps, with an artificial hill and a crater at the end. Whether that is how they moved those rocks or not, I fantasized about it. I saw them on a long walk I took across France and Germany. If *Fitzcarraldo* has a passport and we must list his place of birth, I would list Carnac, in Brittany, where those boulders are one of the miracles of the world.

That ass Erich von Däniken, who writes of the ancient astronomers, cannot believe man is capable of such a feat, but I say give me two years and two thousand men and I will do it all over again for you."

But when you were pulling that ship up the hill, I asked, did you ever question your purpose? Did you wonder if it was all just a little ludicrous?

"There were always low points and lower, and points below the lowest," he said. "I did not allow myself private feelings. I had not the privilege of despair, anxiety, pain. I never paused, I never lost faith, and I have faith enough for fifteen more films."

Fifteen more films like this one?

"I doubt if I or anyone else can make a film like this again," he said. "Film history has shown that this profession of filmmaker has destroyed almost everyone. You can be a cello player until the age of ninety-five. You can be a poet until you die, but the life span of a filmmaker is fifteen years, of making good things. Then they crumble into ashes. I am more than twenty years already. Of course, it has to do with physical strength. For my next project, instead of a film project, I will set out after this film festival is over and walk twenty-five hundred miles on foot."

Where will you go?

He shrugged.

Herzog Defies Death for His Films

MAY 20, 1984

CANNES, FRANCE —This world we live in is a very small place, and if you are lucky the pain and the pleasure are only an airline flight apart. I'm having lunch with Werner Herzog, the West German film director. The day before, he flew into Cannes for the premiere of his new film. Two days before that, he was in the jungles of Nicaragua, talking to a deep-eyed ten-year-old boy carrying an M16 assault rifle. Now we sit in the sunlight, eating fresh strawberries.

Herzog has become the great nomad of modern film directors. He has hardly made a film in Germany since his early days, preferring to seek out the far corners of the Earth, where people make desperate settlements with nature, the gods, and their own weaknesses. All of his movies are about characters who are obsessed by great visions, and none of his characters is more obsessed than Herzog himself. This is why, for some years, he has been the most interesting filmmaker at work in the world.

Consider the three films that currently occupy his attention. The one he has just finished, *Where the Green Ants Dream*, had its premiere Monday as an official selection at the Cannes Film Festival. It is about the confrontation in a godforsaken, heat-baked piece of Australian outback between a uranium-mining company and a tribe of Aborigines who believe that the land must not be disturbed, because it is the place where the green ants dream, and if the ants are awakened, the world will end.

In Nicaragua, Herzog just finished a documentary about a tribe of Mesquito Indians who took up arms against the government of Somoza ("the first time they have fought since the Spanish conquest") and fought for the revolutionary Sandinistas. They are now being maltreated by the Sandinistas, Herzog says, because of their naive belief that they own their ancestral homelands. In a way, this is the same fight being waged by the Aborigines in *Where the Green Ants Dream*.

In nine days Herzog will fly to Pakistan to shoot a film on the upper slopes of K2, one of the highest mountains in the world. He hopes to make a feature film on top of a mountain, and considers this project to be a "training film" to teach him how to survive and use camera equipment at high altitudes and freezing temperatures. Today he sits in the sunlight. A waiter pours chilled wine into his glass, he has had the chicken and the French fries, and now the season's first strawberries are set before him. Elsewhere in Cannes, other directors are screening their new films—movies about third-rate superheroes, sex-crazed stewardesses, and dead teenagers. He does not care, he says, whether his film wins a festival prize or not: "Prizes are for horses."

In *Where the Green Ants Dream*, he comes closer than usual to telling his story in a straightforward narrative way. Usually his films proceed with the logic of dreams. In the outback, a mining company hopes to set off a series of explosions and listen to their echoes, in an attempt to pinpoint likely places for uranium. The Aborigines sit passively on the sites of their explosions, refusing to move, insisting that the ants must not be awakened. We meet characters on both sides: the tall, gangly mining engineer, the implacable tribal leaders, the supercilious president of the mining company.

As usual, Herzog finds strong images to dramatize his story. In *Green Ants*, we see an old white woman waiting patiently in the outback, an opened can of dog food on the ground in front of her, waiting for her pet dog to return from being lost in a mine shaft. We see a group of Aborigines sitting in the aisle of a supermarket, on the place where the last tree in the district once stood, the tree where the tribal men traditionally gathered to "dream" their children before conceiving them. We see a lunar landscape with hundreds of pyramids—leftovers from mineral mines—strewn all the way to the horizon. We do not see any ants.

"I shot the film in only twenty-eight days," Herzog says, "but I had been thinking about it since 1975, when I first visited Australia. I did not think of it as pro-Aborigine, or anti–mining company, but simply about a conflict between two sets of values. In fact, the 'beliefs' of the Aborigines in the film are not their beliefs, but mine: I made up all of their legends about green ants and tribal trees, because I would not presume to make a movie about their real beliefs. It would take me years to understand them. The film is not anthropologically correct about Aborigines, or biologically correct about green ants."

The real conflict in the film seems to be between people who sit and wait, inspired by deep currents of faith, and those who are always in motion, convinced that success lies through industry and activity. As the mining company and the Australian court system race through a dizzying series of "negotiations" and court bearings, the Aborigines, bemused, listen to their dreams—and so does the immaculately dressed little old lady, who waits beneath a parasol for her pet to return.

Herzog's previous film was *Fitzcarraldo*, an awesome undertaking that told the story of a man determined to drag a steamship overland from one river system to another and make his fortune selling rubber from the interior of South America. He wanted to use the rubber to build an opera house in the jungle. The story of Herzog's struggle to make the film, and his insistence on dragging a real ship up a real hill, has become the stuff of legend—and of a harrowing documentary by Les Blank, *Burden of Dreams*, in which Herzog seems half-mad as he explains his plans in the jungle while poisoned arrows pick off his men, planes crash, and engineers tell him the cables on the ship will snap and decapitate everybody.

As Herzog talks about the film he has just finished in Nicaragua, it sounds even more dangerous. Without any credentials or permissions to be in Nicaragua at all, he flew to Honduras and slipped across the border with a small film crew and a bodyguard unit he describes, somewhat cryptically, as "four crack sharpshooters." They worked behind the guerrilla lines in the civil war, filming the story of a Mesquito

Indian tribe that originally backed the Sandinistas against the Somoza regime, but is now—Herzog charges—being fought by the Sandinistas.

Typically, Herzog did not make his film for political reasons, and he says he is not much interested in the political situation in Nicaragua. It was the dynamic of the conflict that attracted him.

"I met a little child with an assault rifle. 'What's your name?' I asked. I learned his name and his village, and that his brothers had been killed and he was avenging them. Later, I saw a young girl, about fifteen, leave the village in the morning with a rifle, and return at night triumphant, because she had traded it for a chicken. To talk about this in political or military terms is insane. It is about a traditional culture being ripped apart by the introduction of instruments of killing. Without the technology—the rifles, from both East and West—it might still be a war, but then the newspapers could not see it."

$$(107)$$

His working title for the film, he said, is *The Ballad of the Mesquitos*. It will be organized around music and will not be a political documentary or even an informational film in any conventional sense.

"I don't know if we were in any great danger or not," Herzog says. "The important thing is not to stick our head up at the wrong time. Our four bodyguards were under strict orders not to shoot, because in the jungle any fire draws return fire. We did not care about protecting the camera or the film. If we had been directly attacked by bayonets, he would have shot back."

"I keep thinking," I tell him, "that someday I will have to write your obituary." I mention his troubles filming *Fitzcarraldo*, and the legendary time he took a crew onto a Caribbean island to make a film about the only man who stayed behind on the slopes of a volcano about to explode. "You seem to seek out danger almost deliberately," I say.

"I am not seeking danger," Herzog says, "I am just seeking my stories."

He says he will stay in Cannes for a day or two and see some movies, before leaving for K2.

Herzog Finds Truth beyond Fact

SEPTEMBER 29, 1998

There is no such thing as a casual conversation with Werner Herzog. When I run into him at a film festival my heart quickens, because I know I am going to be told amazing things, all delivered with the intense air that we are sharing occult knowledge.

Here he is sitting in front of me at the Telluride Film Festival, next to Andre Gregory, of *My Dinner with Andre*. If Andre had dinner with Werner, it would last a week.

Herzog's latest film *Little Dieter Needs to Fly* opens Friday in Chicago at Facets. It is the story of a German who joined the US Air Force, was shot down in Vietnam, and underwent jungle experiences so harrowing that at one point he essentially invited a snake to devour him, and the snake declined.

Herzog himself always looks as if he has just trekked out of the rain forest, and often he has. "You look thin," I told him.

"I returned a week ago from Peru," the German director said, nodding. "I lost twenty pounds. I hacked my way through the jungle. I am making a film about a doomed aircraft flight that I was almost a passenger on. It was the day before Christmas. I paid twenty dollars to the clerk as a bribe. She promised me I had a seat. But this airline, almost all of their planes were grounded, and in the rush I did not get my seat after all.

"The plane went down in the jungle. After a week the search was called off. After eleven and a half days, a young girl crawled out of the jungle. She was the only survivor. I took her back to the site of the crash, which was very hard to find. At the same time, I revisited the locations of my movies *Aguirre, the Wrath of God* and *Fitzcarraldo*— where I pulled the steamship through the jungle."

He shrugged. "All overgrown now. No sign that anyone was ever there."

Both of those films starred Klaus Kinski, he of the fearsome countenance, who fought bitterly with Herzog. There is a story that Herzog pulled a gun on Kinski and ordered him to work or be killed. There is also the story (documented in Les Blank's documentary *Burden of Dreams*) that Herzog refused to use models and special effects. He insisted on building a real steamship and really pulling it through the real jungle with real ropes and winches, and when the German engineers predicted that the ropes would snap and whip around and cut everyone in two, Herzog simply sent the engineers home.

"A native Indian offered to kill Kinski for me," Herzog told me, as we still stood in the aisle at Telluride. "Which I had to decline, because I needed him."

A few years ago at Telluride, Herzog showed me tapes of two recent documentaries he had made, one about the Jesuses of Russia— men who dress as Jesus and walk the streets—and another about villagers who believe that if they crawl out onto a lake when the ice is still thin enough, they can see the angels who live in the city under the water.

They were both astonishing documentaries. The Jesuses reminded me of the story in Salman Rushdie's novel *The Moor's Last Sigh* about the Lenins of Russia—actors who dressed as Lenin and recited his memorized speeches, so peasants could get the message in the age before television. The difference between the Lenins and the Jesuses is that the Lenins presumably existed but the Jesuses were made up. Herzog's "documentary" was fiction.

Herzog moves freely through the spheres of fact, fiction, legend, myth, and invention. He is the first to tell you that not every detail of *Little Dieter Needs to Fly* is ice-cold documentary fact. Yes, that is really Dieter on the screen, and yes, he was really shot down in Vietnam and underwent horrifying experiences. But his image of Death as a jellyfish? "I found it for him," Herzog says.

He is willing to push beyond documentary fact, he says, in his quest for underlying truth.

"The weakness of cinema verité documentaries is that they can never go any deeper. They can only reach the surface of what constitutes truth in cinema. Deeper truth can only be found in poetry, because then you start to fabricate. The world is simply there. It is what men find in it and bring to it that is truth. I am in search of the fathomless."

Was he really scheduled to be a passenger on that doomed flight? I believe him.

A Conversation with Werner Herzog

AUGUST 28, 2005

This is a lightly-edited transcript of an onstage conversation between Werner Herzog and Roger Ebert after the April 2004 screening of Herzog's *Invincible* at Ebert's Overlooked Film Festival at the University of Illinois at Urbana-Champaign. The film involves the story of a Jewish strongman hired to appear as an Aryan god in a vaudeville theater in Germany, at the time of the rise of the Nazi Party.

ROGER EBERT: You know, Werner, some months after I saw this film my wife and I were at the Pritikin Center in Florida, and we made friends with an older couple. We were talking about good films we'd seen and I told him about *Invincible* and I said, "I think the story is true," and he said, "I know it's true because I saw him myself when I was a boy."

WERNER HERZOG: Yes, apparently there was a film once of the real strongman, but only very small fragments seem to remain. I saw something like thirty seconds, which didn't look very interesting at all. The posters are fascinating; the photos are interesting and of course the story was a bit modified. The authentic story actually ends in 1926; Zishe Breitbart died from a rusty nail that he broke through a plank just to show how strong he was. I set the story closer to Hitler's seizing power.

RE: What I admire above all about your film is the ambition of your imagination. You do not make small films and you do not have small ideas. You told me once that our time is starving for lack of images: all the images have been worn out by television and the movies and so we have nothing more to feed our vision. And you come up with images in your film that are so remarkable, including these countless red crabs in this one, that are so frightening to me—because they are life, yet they are mindless and they just keep going on and on despite whatever we think or whatever we hope.

WH: I like the crabs a lot. Actually what you see in the film was shot on Christmas Island, actually two Christmas Islands, one in the Pacific and one in the Indian Ocean west of the Australian mainland. I spent some ten or twelve days just waiting for the crabs to arrive because there's only a very short window of opportunity during the very first days; seventy or eighty million crabs start migrating from the jungle to the beaches. They mate, lay their eggs, and disappear back into the jungle. So it took quite an effort and some time to get them on film.

RE: But what I am amazed by is that no other director making this story, set in Europe, would feel that he had to go to the Indian Ocean to photograph crabs for it. I love the fact that your mind encompasses the . . .

WH: I think about them and I don't know why. I can't explain it. I know there's something very big for example, to see the crabs crossing the railroad tracks, something that I can't explain, but I know there's something big, like for example the dancing chicken at the end of *Stroszek*.

RE: Which is one of my favorites.

WH: It is also one of my great favorites, and that image also fell into my lap. I don't know how and why; the strange thing is that with both the crabs and the dancing chicken at the end of *Stroszek*, the crew couldn't take it, they hated it, they were a loyal group and in case of *Stroszek* they hated it so badly that I had to operate the camera myself because the cinematographer who was very good and dedicated, hated it so much that he didn't want to shoot it. He said, "I've never seen anything as dumb as that." And I tried to say, "You know there's something so big about it." But they couldn't see it.

RE: I have this series of Great Movies reviews that I've been writing;
Aguirre was the first of your movies I wrote about and then I wrote
about *Stroszek*. I'm going to try to quote—I believe there was a
fireman or a police officer who gets on his radio . . .

WH: Yeah.

RE: And he calls for help and he says, "We have a dead man on a . . ."

WH: "We have a dead man on the ski lift, and we have a dancing chicken!
Send us an electrician!"

RE: "Send us an electrician." That film was shot in Wisconsin.

WH: Yes, and the dancing chicken was shot in Cherokee, North Caro-
lina. When you are speaking about these images, there's something
bigger about them, and I keep saying that we do have to develop
an adequate language for our state of civilization, and we do have
to create adequate pictures—images for our civilization. If we do
not do that, we die out like dinosaurs, so it's of a different mag-
nitude, trying to do something against the wasteland of images
that surround us, on television, magazines, postcards, posters in
travel agencies . . .

RE: I see so many movies that are all the same, they're cut off like
sausages, you get another two hours' worth and then you go home
and you forget about them. Your films expand me, they exhilarate
me, they make me feel that you are trying to put your arms around
enormous ideas. And at the same time there's a feeling of hopelessness. I think of Aguirre on the sinking raft, in the middle of the
river, mad, surrounded by gibbering monkeys. And Fitzcarraldo,
who wanted to pull the ship across the mountain into the other
river. Only you would have thought that it would have to be done
with a real ship. It couldn't be models or special effects.

WH: It was disgusting actually because at that time 20th Century Fox
was interested to produce a film and we had a very brief conversation of about five sentences because it was clear their position
was, "You have to do it with a miniature boat." From there on it
was clear no one in the industry would ever support something like
that. It was really risky, and I knew, at that moment, I was alone
with it. I tried to explain that I wanted to have the audience know

that at the most fundamental level it was real. Today when you see mainstream movies, in many moments, even when it's not really necessary, there are special effects. It's a young audience, and at six and seven kids can identify them, they know it was a digital effect, and normally they even know how they were done. But I had the feeling I wanted to put the audience back in the position where they could trust their eyes . . .

RE: It's totally clear in that film that it's a real ship and that the ropes are straining. If you look at *Lord of the Rings* for example, they have people in a chain stretched across mountainsides, and they're obviously special effects. But in *Cobra Verde*, your film in Africa, you had a message that was being passed down a line of people for miles and miles, and it was really happening. The people were there in an endless chain on the hillsides. It's clear that it's really happening, and it's extraordinary.

WH: There is a certain quality that you sense when you move a ship over a mountain. It was 360 tons and I knew I would manage it. But I knew that it would create unsightly things that no one would expect. There were many huge steel cables that are five centimeters in diameter, I mean as thick as this table. They would break like a thin thread. When you tap them before they break, when you touch them and tap them, they sound thick, they sound different, and when they break, there's so much tension, there's so much pressure, that the cable is red hot inside, it's glowing inside. That was one thing I didn't show in the film but I've seen it and many of the things that you see in *Fitzcarraldo* were created by the events themselves. I've always been after the deeper truth, the ecstatic truth, and I will always defend that, as long as there's breath in me.

RE: And you also argue for the real locations. It would have been possible to shoot *Fitzcarraldo* without going nine hundred miles up the Amazon and living with arrows coming out of the jungle that could kill your crew. But you told me once of the voodoo of location; you said you also wanted to use the same locations that Murnau used for *Nosferatu* because of the vibrations . . .

WH: Yes, I said that, but I don't really believe in vibrations; that belongs to the hippie age. There is one shot where a line of buildings is still standing in a city in Northern Germany which I used in much of the film, and since I knew there were a few buildings hidden in the film, I just tried to bow my head in reverence. But otherwise, sure, I'm good with locations. I know how to do it. It is not just buildings; I direct landscapes.

RE: Would you say that Murnau was your true predecessor?

WH: Yes. I believe he certainly was because I'm still convinced that there's no better German film than *Nosferatu*, his silent film, and since we were the first postwar generation and we had no fathers, we had no mentors, we had no teachers, we had no masters, we were a generation of orphans. Many of us actually were orphans. Same thing with me but in many other cases a father just died in captivity, in the war, whatever. And those who make movies, the majority, the vast majority, died with the Nazi regime. A few were sent to concentration camps and the best left the country like Murnau and others, so the only kind of reference in my case was the generation of the grandfathers, the silent era of expressionist films. [The film critic and historian] Lotte Eisner was a great mentor of mine, who knew the entire film history, I mean she knew every single person that had worked in cinema and had an important part. She knew the brothers Lumière, she knew Méliès, who made films between 1904 and 1914, and she knew Eisenstein and all the younger ones. The young friends, the young German ones. So she was one of the very last people on this planet who had known all of them and seen all of their films, and there was not one who did not bow his or her head in reverence to her.

RE: The story that I love is that when you finished your first film, you put it in a knapsack on your back and you walked from Germany to Paris to give it to Lotte Eisner.

WH: No, that is not . . .

RE: Didn't you really do that?

WH: Actually, with *Signs of Life*, my first film, I sent it by mail and she actually saw it and she sent it to Fritz Lang, saying, "Finally they have cinema again in Germany." He liked the film but the story of the walk to Lotte is kind of different. I got a call a couple of years later, a friend calls me and the phone wakes me up early in the morning. And she says, "Come quickly, come quickly, do you sit? Do you sit?" And I just said, "Yes, I'm sitting." "Come quickly, Lotte is dying, she had a massive stroke and she is dying. Come quickly, you must come." So I put the phone down, and I thought for a moment. I said, "I am not going to fly, I refuse to take a plane, refuse to take a car, I refuse to do anything else, I will come on foot," because I didn't want her to die. And I was absolutely convinced—I am not superstitious—I was totally absolutely convinced that while I was walking from Germany to Paris to see her, she would not have a chance to die, I wouldn't allow her to die, I didn't want her to die, it was too early. She was still needed too badly. So that was beginning of winter, that year was really bitter because we had violent storms, snowstorms, rainstorms coming from the west. I took a compass reading and I took the straightest line that I could across fields, across rivers, and I arrived at Paris and she was out of hospital. She was out of hospital and survived. Eight years later, she must have been ninety years, nobody knows exactly how old she was because she started to cheat from seventy-five on, I think she celebrated her seventy-fifth birthday a couple of times. And very casually, we were having tea, and she said to me, nibbling on a cookie, she said to me, "Listen, listen to me, I'm almost blind, I cannot read any more, I cannot see any more films, I cannot walk any more, I'm tired of life"—she actually even said it "sucked" and she was saturated of life—and she said to me, "but there's still this spell on me, that I must not die," and I said to her very casually, "The spell is lifted," and two weeks later she died. And she died at the right time then, it was good, it was good to die then. So I didn't carry a print on my back.

RE: It is a wonderful story.

WH: Actually I do like to carry prints, because it somehow verifies a strange fact which is hard for me to believe. Very often I think I might just be dreaming; could it be my brother who made the film, and I tried to claim that it was me? I don't really know. I had a strange father who didn't impact at all in my life. When I met him once in a while, he was living a completely invented sort of life. He spoke about some sort of universal scientific study that he had written but I knew he had never written one line. And he kept on studying and studying in I don't know how many fields, and he would talk to visitors, even his own boys, to his own children, he would talk about his study, even though we would know he had never written it. And I remember one moment I touched his shoulder and said, "Yes, but you've never written it." And he looked at me and somehow realized in a moment he hadn't written it, but five minutes later he was raving about it again. So very often I think, "Yeah, have I really made films or not?" And I carry a print once in a while; you feel the weight of it, weight like fifty pounds. (117)

RE: You have made the film.

WH: (*Laughs.*) Yeah.

RE: This film *Invincible* begins with the little boy and his relationship with his brother, and him telling the story about the rooster. And that fable sets the stage for the film because this films plays to me like a fable, like one of those stories about giants and strong men and about how they come to the city and how they save the maiden and vanquish the villain. Its simplicity is so beautiful. The hero has a misplaced trust in strength, muscles are not going to be the answer, but his mind, his purity, is so clear about that. The story affects me on a level of fable and allegory.

WH: Yes, I liked the rooster story a lot and I knew it had to be in the film. It's good to open the film like that. And of course what makes a lot of difference in stories like this is, he's in love with the young pianist, but there's an equal love story with his younger brother. In something like, I don't know exactly, like fifty films, I've never filmed a kiss. And in this film all of a sudden it's a very tender, very fleeting kiss. I've never done a kiss in my life in a movie. Nor telephone calls, do they occur in my movies. People driving in cars do not affect me much; very few times do you see people driving. In a few of my films you see some cars. It probably reflects the fact that I grew up in a very remote place, the most remote place in the Alps mountains, and until I was eleven I had not seen films, I actually did not even know of the existence of movies. And we would run when we saw a motorcar. Like in the film, we would really run when a motorcar was passing, we wanted to look. I made my first phone call at the age of seventeen.

RE: I don't want to prompt you with another story that I probably have wrong, but when you mention being eleven, I'm trying to remember the details of something you told me once of having seen Klaus Kinski. When you were young.

WH: I was thirteen then.

RE: Thirteen. And knowing, somehow. You saw him and you knew something.

WH: We had moved to Munich, and we lived in some sort of a boarding house, the four of us, my mother and my two brothers, so it was four persons in one room. One day, the owner of the place, an elderly lady who had a heart for starving artists, picked up Kinski literally from the street, well, actually from an attic that he had occupied, he had squatted in an attic and filled it up with autumn leaves, and made huge scandals, and would climb up to the roof and defy policemen who would try to arrest him. And she picked him up and fed him and gave him a very small room in our boarding house. She did his laundry, fed him, everything, for free. And from the very first moment I was terrorized. Everyone was in sheer terror. It took him only forty-eight hours and the entire bathroom was in smithereens.

He would yell and scream, and the only one that was not afraid— who was just in amazement and wonderment—was a young peasant women, something like seventeen or eighteen years old. She was not afraid at all and she had a tray and Kinski flung the tray against the wall and all the dishes left a mess and I still see her, she bends down, slowly picks up the empty tray, and smacks him in the face with it. And he would calm down for a moment, but it was only fleeting, because he would be like, how should I say, like a hurricane. Laying waste to apartments, movies, he would wreck cars, he would wreck Ferraris, no it was not Ferraris, it was Rolls-Royces, at a rate of a Rolls-Royce a week.

Later when he was in Italy and earned a lot of money, there was always a trail of devastation behind him, and some of it was not funny because part of him was really, really, really bad. So he may rest in peace and make his peace with the creator if ever he encounters him. So then I was thirteen. And of course one day I asked him to do *Aguirre*. When I sent him the screenplay, twelve years later, I knew if he would accept it, what I had to expect, but I was never afraid.

RE: Many directors do not hire someone that they believe is going to be trouble.

WH: No, it was much more.

RE: It was much more than trouble. You were going take him into the middle of the rain forest hundreds of miles from anything and live with him there for months. And it was a film that you could not possibly start again if anything went wrong. And you bet everything on that. When we think of *Aguirre* we think of Kinski, so yours was the right decision, but what a chance you took.

WH: When you know that there is only one option that you have, there is no alternative. There is absolutely no alternative. But Kinski doing Aguirre must not be afraid of actually doing it, and no matter what comes along you will prevail as long as it's a secure vision.

RE: The legend is that Kinski accepted movies entirely on the basis of convenience and location.

WH: Money.

RE: Money.

WH: He would even do hard-core pornos for money. Money, money, money! And if for any reason he would start to scream, he would scream until he had frost on his mouth. He would scream about this pig who didn't offer him decent money, who was this psychopathic asshole. Obviously he made some distinctions, because I obviously paid him much less than others would offer him. I mean a fraction of that. I didn't have the budget. Kinski the bastard won a third of the entire budget.

And then, there's an interesting thing, the real good version is the German version, it's the authentic version, but since we filmed a lot in rapids there was such a huge noise that—of course we did have some direct sound—but you could hardly understand a word. We had to post-synch it, so I said to Klaus, "We need you for loop-ing, for one and a half days." He said, "Yes, I'm coming, but it will cost a million dollars." And there was absolutely no way. He knew, of course, I didn't have a thousand dollars, everything was gone, my wristwatch was gone, everything, and he asked for a million dollars, he hated the film so badly you could not believe it. And he didn't show up for looping so I looped it with a different voice, and the voice is as good as Kinski. I took a lot of effort; nobody, nobody would ever know. But you know it now. Can you please not . . . do not leak to the press.

(120)

RE: But you have just told 1,600 people. (*Laughter*.) What is astonish-ing, you returned to the jungle for *Fitzcarraldo*, and it seemed like you both wanted to do this.

WH: We were not mad I think. He understood that there was a higher duty that both of us had to accept. That was actually the most dan-gerous of all, because of course I could tolerate all sorts of things, and it was not only Kinski that was hard to take. Moving the ship over the hill was something you could not imagine, and we had all sorts of catastrophes. We had two plane crashes. We had people shot with huge arrows at the throat that almost killed them and we operated on them on kitchen tables. Everything in the book happened, with now Kinski on this location. Everyone in the crew after two days would turn against me: "How can you have the guts to bring in this pestilence again? We are refusing!" The actors on a daily basis would threaten to terminate with a strike. For me there was one borderline, it was duty, a high duty. High duty on which he stood and I stood.

In *Aguirre*, at the end, ten days before the end of shooting, Kin-ski, I believe as usual, didn't learn his lines. They were very short lines anyway, and he all of a sudden interrupts everything and throws everything around and he screams in a tantrum and destroys half the set and screams that the still photographer had smiled and had to be dismissed on the spot. Of course I wouldn't dismiss him because everyone else would have walked out in solidarity.

I said "No, I'm not doing it, let's calm down and we'll continue." And he left the set. And I knew why he had done it because he had done it thirty-five times just within the last five years. And because of that, movies were canceled and destroyed. It was too well-documented. He packed his things into a speedboat and screamed and screamed. And it was somehow not correctly reported in the press, but I have witnesses that I was unarmed, and did not point a gun at him, but I walked up and I said to him, "Klaus, I don't have to make up my mind. I've had months of deliberating where is the borderline that we will not transgress. This would be the transgression, the borderline. This is something that you will not survive." (121)

I said to him, "I do have a rifle," very calmly. He could try to take the boat and he might reach the next bend of the river but he would have eight bullets through his head. But of course there were nine bullets, and I said, "Guess who gets the last one?" And he looked at me and he understood it was not a joke anymore. I would have done it. He understood he better behave, and it was kind of hostile for the next couple of days. But what I'm trying to say is, the incident may sound funny now, and it seems funny and bizarre to me; if I sat out there I would laugh with you. But what I'm trying to say is that there's always been a very clear borderline, a line that must not be stepped over. So once you accept the duty you have to understand the duty that is upon you. I've always understood it myself.

RE: In *Invincible* you have the opposite kind of actor; I think your star [Jouko Ahola] was actually from Scandinavia.

WH: Twice he was named the strongest man in the world.

RE: He seems like the sweetest man alive, and his smile is so warm.

WH: He is the opposite of Kinski; he's a very sweet man. And you could tell instantly, the first moment that you would see the man, you have that feeling in a particular woman's sense, you sense the confidence and weakness of the man, from five miles away. No it's true, they love him. And he somehow had a way with for example with Anna Gourari, who plays the pianist in Tim Roth's show.

The strongman was reluctant to accept the role, because he'd never been in a movie and he said, "Well, can I do that?" and I said, "Yes, you can do it. I know my job and I know how to make you into a convincing actor; you just have to have the confidence in your physical strength and you have to have the confidence in who you are. And you should trust your own eyes, so if you lift nine hundred pounds off the ground, you believe it is actually nine hundred pounds."

He showed up and he can lift more, so-called dead lifting. He bowed down and lifted it up off the ground on to his knees and he held it up in Los Angeles, where all the muscle men are working out, including Schwarzenegger, a hundred of them. He brought his own bar because he needs an elongated bar to put on weight after weight after weight. And he does that, he starts pumping iron and they surround him and then he has nearly four hundred men around him and just staring at the thousand pounds. He crouches down. Lifts it, drops it, walks away, and takes a shower.

RE: And at the opposite end of the physical scale, Tim Roth, the ninety-pound weakling, one of the best actors in the world.

WH: Yes he is, yes he is.

RE: The sensation I've had each time I see the film is that if I wanted to, if I didn't actually didn't decide not to, I would be hypnotized by him. He's looking directly at me through the screen.

WH: That's actually happened, I taught him how to hypnotize, because I did once an entire feature film that . . .

RE: *Heart of Glass*!

WH: *Heart of Glass*, yes, I did that film with the entire cast under hypnosis. And so I taught Tim Roth how to do it and the funny thing was that the cinematographer was looking through the eyepiece and sitting that close and all of a sudden started to weave, and I grabbed him by the hair while the scene was still running and softly shook him. So yes, if the audience will be willing, it can be hypnotized from the screen. And that was what I actually had planned to do in *Heart of Glass*; I actually had the idea that I would appear on screen myself, and explain that I was the director and the scenes were shot under hypnosis. "And if you are willing to see the film under hypnosis, you should follow my advice now. I will ask you to look at something like a pencil, and don't remove your eyes, and listen to my voice and follow my words and follow my instructions."

And of course I would tell the audience that at the end of the film they will return to the screen and softly wake up again. I have actually shown films to audiences who were hypnotized, including for example *Aguirre*. With *Aguirre* it was very strange because I remember that one young women who saw the film was constantly circling around *Aguirre* as if she was a helicopter and she could see behind.

RE: *Heart of Glass* is a great film about a community that loses the secret of making rose-tinted glass.

WH: Ruby glass.

RE: Ruby glass that has sustained this community for many generations. The shot that I always remember is the two guys looking at each other from across the table and drinking beer and one reaches up and breaks his beer stein over the other one's head. And the other one makes no reaction.

WH: Yeah, but I've seen things like that when I grew up in the country, and I could predict that in ten minutes there would be a fight. And they would be all quiet and just stare at each other. I would know the ritual of how they would finally take up the steins and break them over each other's heads. Actually in Bavaria there's a law that there must be two grooves on either side of a stein so that it breaks easier when you hit, because it can fracture your skull.

RE: It is impossible to ask you anything without being fascinated by the answer. It's 2 a.m. and no one has left; you've got them hypnotized.

WH: It's gotten very late.

"Tell Me about the Iceberg,
Tell Me about Your Dreams"

JULY 7, 2008

Werner Herzog's documentary *Encounters at the End of the World* is a film about the humans and other creatures who make their homes at the South Pole. It opens July 11 at the Music Box and is in release around the world. I posed five questions to the great director.

ROGER EBERT: From the beginning of your career, you have been drawn to people who exist at the extremes. It is impossible to conceive of a Herzog film about ordinary people living ordinary lives. Why are the exceptions so much the rule with you?

WERNER HERZOG: I am curious about our human condition. As you would understand the very nature of physical matter by putting it under extreme temperature, pressure, or radiation, similarly human beings would reveal their nature under extreme conditions. The Greeks have a proverbial saying I always liked: "A captain only shows during a storm." Ordinary lives are the ones we lead, but they are not really a fertile soil for movies.

RE: From the day of *Aguirre* and even earlier, you have been drawn to far-off, isolated places. The working conditions for some of your shoots must be extremely difficult. Your reason for filming in the rain forest is famous; you said you filmed hundreds of miles up the Amazon (instead of a few miles into the jungle) because the films would absorb "the voodoo of the locations." Now here you are at the South Pole. What draws you to the end of the world?

WH: As I grew up in a very isolated place in the mountains of Bavaria, there has always been an enormous curiosity within me about what lay beyond the horizon. The locations of *Aguirre* were quite obvious. But the opinion that during the filming of *Fitzcarraldo* I rejected the idea of filming near our headquarters in the jungle city of Iquitos in order to get some "voodoo" is certainly wrong, and hard to get out of the public perception.

Fitzcarraldo depended on a specific geography: two parallel tributaries of the Amazon had to come within less than a mile of each other with only a manageable mountain in between for hauling a boat across. I started out at one of the suitable locations in northern Peru close to the border with Ecuador, but once I had my camp for about one thousand extras completed, a border war broke out, and the camp was burnt to the ground. The next best location was more than a thousand kilometers from Iquitos, and I had no real choice.

As for the South Pole, it itself has no specific attraction for me. It was incredible underwater footage from under the ice of the Ross Sea that made Antarctica irresistible. But if I had a chance to venture out with a camera to a planet in our solar system, I would go, even if it were a one-way ticket only.

RE: What was your method? All of the people you talk to in *Encounters at the End of the World* are genuinely interesting originals, with a particular way of discussing their lives almost objectively. Did you wander around chatting up your South Pole citizens? How did they regard the idea of a film about their settlement? Did some of them know you and your work? Among those who did not, how did you strike them?

WH: Going to Antarctica required a lot of self-confidence. There was no possibility to go on a scouting trip. I went down there only with a cinematographer (I did the production sound), and I knew I had to come back with a film seven weeks later.

The community at McMurdo did not know much about me, but they accepted me quickly. Quite a few of them I met only for a few minutes more than what you can see on the screen. The scientist who studies the gigantic glaciers ("larger than the country that built the Titanic") was on his way to his plane to New Zealand; he had only thirty minutes for me, and twenty I spent to make him feel calm and comfortable. Then I said: "I know that deep inside you are a poet. Tell me about the iceberg, and tell me about your dreams."

RE: From where do you draw your boundless energy and curiosity? Although you are often cut off from most of the usual sources of financing for films, you remain one of the most prolific and productive of all directors, and never, ever, compromise your principles to make a merely "commercial" project.

WH: I can only take a guess. I have always followed a vision, and developed a sense of duty. The best answer about my curiosity comes from one of the characters in *Encounters*, the Bulgarian man who drives a Caterpillar. He studied philosophy and comparative literature, and tells about his grandmother who read the Odyssey to him as a child. "That's when I fell in love with the world," he says, and my heart stood still for a moment. I knew I had fallen in love with the world as well when I was very young, and all my films are my witness. As to "merely commercial" projects: I always wanted to do mainstream films, films that could be understood in all countries, by all ages. I may have become some sort of a secret mainstream with some of my films. And as to finances: only faith moves mountains, and money does not.

RE: You strike in this film once again an apocalyptic note. The title could have a double meaning. Do you feel we are living at the end of days? If you do, what is the purpose for continuing to make movies, or work at all, or care? How do you feel about the possibility of the annihilation of all of your work, and all the other expressions of mankind over the centuries?

WH: I made some other films with an apocalyptic note, *Lessons of Darkness* most notably, and *Fata Morgana*. However, I do not think that the end is imminent, but one thing is clear: we are only fugitive guests on our planet. Martin Luther, the reformer, was asked: "What would you do, if the world came to an end tomorrow?" and he replied, "I would plant an apple tree." I would start shooting a new film.

The Ecstasy of the Filmmaker Herzog

APRIL 6, 2010

I saw *Aguirre, the Wrath of God* for the first time in a defrocked Lutheran Church in the Lincoln Park neighborhood, which Milos Stehlik had taken over for his newly-born Facets Multimedia. "It is a film you must see," he told me. "Bring a pillow. The pews can get hard."

I saw a great film, one of the greatest ever made. An essential film. In 1999, I made it one of the first titles in my Great Movies collection. Now I wonder if I really saw it at all.

Werner Herzog is in Boulder this week, to join another great director, Ramin Bahrani, in viewing *Aguirre* a shot at a time. It is a lifetime experience for a film lover. We're at the 62nd annual Conference on World Affairs. Maybe a thousand people crowded into Macky Auditorium, where Bahrani and Herzog sat side by side in the dark, Jim Emerson froze the DVD frames when required, people shouted out questions, and Herzog spoke about the making of the film.

This program was born in 2009. Last year, Bahrani joined us for a "Cinema Interruptus" of his *Chop Shop*. He spoke of film with such respect and love. He is a meticulous director; not a frame is filmed with inattention. He mentioned how much he would love to meet Herzog. An idea was born. This year Ramin and I invited Herzog to join us. Herzog came, and was mesmerizing. I could listen to him all night. His imagination is not beaten dead by popular culture. He seeks new visions—literally, at the poles, in the deserts, in the sea, on mountaintops, and in the human mind. Here he was discussing his experiences in filming the first seventeen minutes of *Aguirre*, for that's as far as we got on the first day of the week.

The film opens with a shot of perhaps two hundred Spanish con-quistadores and Indian slaves, making their way down a narrow path with a two thousand meter drop on either side. They drag cannon and supplies. It is muddy and slippery. Only half a dozen were professional actors. The others were native Indians or hippies and street people recruited in the nearest small city. He sent them up the path in the reverse order that he wanted them to descend. Were they happy to wait up there? The path was too narrow for two to pass. If he held up the line at the bottom, they had no choice.

They descend at first in a very long shot, indistinct in the mist, dwarfed by the Peruvian rain forest. Then, in the same unbroken shot, the camera adjusting, we see them appear in foreground, moving from left to right. Right, the positive direction, because they believe they are approaching El Dorado. Not professional faces. Weathered, tired, lived-in faces. The Indians wear the clothes they were wearing when they arrived at the shoot.

Herzog had only one take. He would never be able to persuade his actors to climb again for a second one. As we watched them descend, he froze the DVD frame to discuss several of the actors. A fat man who ate all the mangos. A close friend, semiliterate, who had bicycled thirty-five thousand kilometers around North America and later became a great photographer. Above all, his star Klaus Kinski, about whom some years later he made a film: *My Best Fiend*.

Kinski, in constant rage. Describing himself as a "natural man" who could live in the forest like an animal. Then complaining that his tent leaked. Then complaining that the thatch shelter built over the tent leaked. Then moving at great inconvenience to the production into a shabby hotel where he beat his wife nightly, the crew discreetly removing the blood stains.

"A coward," Herzog says.

"Is it true," a voice from the dark asks, "that the Indians asked your permission to murder him?"

"No. That was on *Fitzcarraldo*."

Bahrani freezes a frame showing a small covered carrier like a tent, borne through the jungle on poles by bearers. It contains one of the women in the party. This detail, and most of the film, has no real basis in fact. Everything comes from Herzog's imagination.

"Is that your hand?" Bahrani asks. We see a bare hand shoot out to steady the carrier, and then disappear.

"Yes, that is my appearance in the film, "Herzog says. "I was afraid they would lose their footing."

"When I show this film to my students at Columbia," Bahrani says, "I always tell them, I'll bet that's Herzog's hand."

The party arrives at the Urubamba River, with its famous rapids. It is January 2, 1971—flood season. They construct rafts so that an advance party, led by Aguirre, can go on ahead. They can only film the river scenes once, because the jungle makes it impossible to walk back along its banks. One of the rafts is deliberately steered into an eddy. This was very dangerous, Herzog says; they had men above them on a cliff with ropes to lower if the raft capsized. Only the toughest of the actors were on this raft, "with a very substantial increase in pay."

A quarter mile upstream from this shot, Herzog says, he returned only a year ago to the Urubamba to shoot a scene for his latest film *My Son, My Son, What Have Ye Done*. Nobody asked him why, and indeed it is hard to pinpoint a reason why footage from a Peruvian rapids was required for a crime drama set in San Diego. Somehow, with Herzog, you don't ask such a question.

There were other problems. Herzog grabbed a tree that was a highway for fire ants, then hit the tree with his machete and dislodged hundreds more that fell upon him. A thieving transportation company bribed customs officials to stamp its documents, and then dumped the cans of negative in a field, where Herzog's brother later discovered and rescued them. Herzog shot the second half of the film not knowing if he had the negative of the first half.

He said he doesn't give a great deal of thought to composition. "I focus entirely on the subject of the shot." One shot shows the fat man straddling a cannon and eating a mango. A voice asks, "Is that a phallic symbol?" Herzog replies, "It honestly never occurred to me until you pointed it out. I wanted to have a shot showing the man who consumed all our mangos."

There is audience discussion of the "painterly composition" of a shot of a camp the Spanish party makes in a clearing.

"I am a filmmaker, not a painter," Herzog says. "I have a gift for arranging men and horses. It comes easy for me."

It is 6 p.m., and we have been through only seventeen minutes of the film. Herzog can spare only one more day away from his current film. Then Bahrani will take over, and after him, Jim Emerson and the actress Julia Sweeney. Many of those in the audience are old hands at this process. They are amazingly well-informed.

Herzog must return to work. He has been granted three hours to film inside the Cave of Chauvet-Pont-d'Arc in Southern France, where the wall paintings have been dated to thirty-two thousand years ago. There is no documentarian better suited than Herzog to make this film of a sacred place unseen for centuries. He will bring to it awe and poetry.

I said earlier I wondered if I had ever truly *seen Aguirre, the Wrath of God*. I've seen it many times, and analyzed it a shot at a time. But I realize that to some degree I saw it through eyes conditioned by commercial movies.

Herzog has spoken of the "voodoo of location." By that I think he means the ways in which an actual location, where actual events take place, carries a psychic, or emotional, or sensory, charge to the screen. There are no special effects at all in *Aguirre*. What you see is what was actually there. Many of the shots were done in one take. Some two. Only a few dialogue passages in three or four. In some cases, the events shown could only take place one time.

The film documents a daring and inspirational enterprise, and a reckless one. It shows Europeans invading a new land, tragically unsuited to survive in it and ruinous to the existing culture. They searched for gold—which, in some way, explains all colonialism. But Herzog said, "I give no thought to symbols or messages." He also has only contempt for story arc, "the Hollywood hero going through a pleasing series of events." Nor does he care about time, and he is

willing to let a shot extend beyond its conventional length if the dura-
tion creates a feeling within us.

It is all the experience itself, the immediate experience. During
some of the scenes on the river rafts, he said, "we were all joined
together—actors and crew members—and we knew we could only
do this one time." What they did put their lives at risk, although no
one died. They did it for many reasons. Then it was done. Now we
see the film. The film, and also the record of the creation of a vision.

Part 4 The Great Movies

Aguirre, the Wrath of God

APRIL 4, 1999 (RELEASED 1972)

On this river God never finished his creation.

The captured Indian speaks solemnly to the last remnants of a Spanish expedition seeking the fabled El Dorado, the city of gold. A padre hands him a Bible, "the word of God." He holds it to his ear but can hear nothing. Around his neck hangs a golden bauble. The Spanish rip it from him and hold it before their eyes, mesmerized by the hope that now, finally, at last, El Dorado must be at hand. "Where is the city?" they cry at the Indian, using their slave as an interpreter. He waves his hand vaguely at the river. It is further. Always further.

Werner Herzog's *Aguirre, the Wrath of God* is one of the great haunting visions of the cinema. It tells the story of the doomed expedition of the conquistador Gonzalo Pizarro, who in 1560 and 1561 led a body of men into the Peruvian rain forest, lured by stories of the lost city. The opening shot is a striking image: a long line of men snakes its way down a steep path to a valley far below, while clouds of mist obscure the peaks. These men wear steel helmets and breastplates and carry their women in enclosed sedan chairs. They are dressed for a court pageant, not for the jungle.

The music sets the tone. It is haunting, ecclesiastical, human, and yet something else. It is by Florian Fricke, whose band Popol Vuh (named for the Mayan creation myth) has contributed the soundtracks to many Herzog films. For this opening sequence, Herzog told me, "We used a strange instrument, which we called a 'choir-organ.' It has inside it three dozen different tapes running parallel to each other in loops. . . . All these tapes are running at the same time, and there is a keyboard on which you can play them like an organ so that [it will] sound just like a human choir but yet, at the same time, very artificial and really quite eerie."

I emphasize the music because the sound of a Herzog film is organically part of its effect. His stories begin in a straightforward manner, but their result is incalculable, and there is no telling where they may lead: they conclude not in an "ending" but in the creation of a mood within us—a spiritual or visionary feeling. I believe he wants his audiences to feel like detached observers, standing outside time, saddened by the immensity of the universe as it bears down on the dreams and delusions of man.

If the music is crucial to *Aguirre, the Wrath of God*, so is the face of Klaus Kinski. He has haunted blue eyes and wide, thick lips that would look sensual if they were not pulled back in the rictus of madness. Here he plays the strongest-willed of the conquistadors. Herzog told me that he was a youth in Germany when he saw Kinski for the first time: "At that moment I knew it was my destiny to make films, and his to act in them."

When Pizarro fears that his expedition is a folly, he selects a small party to spend a week exploring farther upriver. If they find nothing, he says, the attempt will be abandoned. This smaller party is led by the aristocrat Don Pedro de Ursua, with Aguirre (Kinski) as his second-in-command. Also in the party, along with soldiers and slaves, are a priest, Gaspar de Carvajal; the fatuous nobleman Fernando de Guzman; Ursua's wife, Flores; Aguirre's daughter Inez; and a black slave named Okello, who sadly tells one of the women, "I was born a prince, and men were forbidden to look on me. Now I am in chains."

Herzog does not hurry their journey or fill it with artificial episodes of suspense and action. What we feel above all is the immensity of the river and the surrounding forest—which offers no shore to stand on because the waters have risen and flooded it. Consider how Herzog handles an early crisis, when one of the rafts is caught in a whirlpool. The slaves row furiously, but the raft cannot move. Herzog's camera stays across the river from the endangered rafters; their distress seems distant and insoluble. Aguirre contemptuously dismisses any attempt to rescue them, but a party is sent out to try to reach them from the other side. In the morning, the raft still floats in place; everyone on it is dead.

How did they die? I have an idea, but so do you. The point is that death is the destiny of this expedition. Ursua, the leader, is put under arrest. Aguirre arranges the selection of Guzman as their new leader. Soon both are dead. Guzman's last meal is fish and fruit, which as acting "emperor" he eats greedily while his men count out a few kernels of corn apiece. A horse goes mad, he orders it thrown overboard, and men mutter darkly that it would have supplied meat for a week. Guzman's dead body is found soon after.

(137)

Aguirre rules with a reign of terror. He stalks about the raft with a curious lopsided gait, as if one of his knees will not bend. There is madness in his eyes. When he overhears one of the men whispering of plans to escape, he cuts off his head so swiftly that the dead head finishes the sentence it was speaking. Death occurs mostly offscreen in the film, or swiftly and silently, as arrows fly softly out of the jungle and into the necks and backs of the men. The film's final images, among the most memorable I have ever seen, are of Aguirre alone on his raft, surrounded by corpses and by hundreds of chattering little monkeys, still planning his new empire.

The filming of *Aguirre* is a legend in film circles. Herzog, a German director who speaks of the "voodoo of location," took his actors and crew into a remote jungle district where fever was frequent and starvation seemed like a possibility. It is said Herzog held a gun on Kinski to force him to continue acting, although Kinski, in his autobiography, denies this, adding darkly that he had the only gun. The actors, crew members, and cameras were all actually on rafts like those we see, and often, Herzog told me, "I did not know the dialogue ten minutes before we shot a scene."

The film is not driven by dialogue, anyway, or even by the characters, except for Aguirre, whose personality is created as much by Kinski's face and body as by words. What Herzog sees in the story, I think, is what he finds in many of his films: men haunted by a vision of great achievement, who commit the sin of pride by daring to reach for it, and are crushed by an implacable universe. One thinks of his documentary about the ski jumper Steiner, who wanted to fly forever, and became so good that he was in danger of overshooting the landing area and crushing himself against stones and trees.

Of modern filmmakers, Werner Herzog is the most visionary and the most obsessed with great themes. Little wonder that he has directed many operas. He does not want to tell a plotted story or record amusing dialogue; he wants to lift us up into realms of wonder. Only a handful of modern films share the audacity of his vision; I think of *2001: A Space Odyssey* and *Apocalypse Now*.

Among active directors, the one who seems as messianic is Oliver Stone. There is a kind of saintly madness in the way they talk about their work; they cannot be bothered with conventional success, because they reach for transcendence.

The companion film to *Aguirre* is Herzog's *Fitzcarraldo*, also starring Kinski, also shot in the rain forest, also about an impossible task: a man who physically wants to move a steamship from one river system to another by dragging it across land. Of course Herzog literally dragged a real ship across land to make the film, despite urgent warnings by engineers that the cables would snap and slice everyone in half. A documentary about the shooting of that film, *Burden of Dreams*, by Les Blank, is as harrowing as the film itself.

The Enigma of Kaspar Hauser

NOVEMBER 17, 2007 (RELEASED 1974)

Werner Herzog's films do not depend on "acting" in the conventional sense. He is most content when he finds an actor who embodies the essence of a character, and he studies that essence with a fascinated intensity. Consider the case of Bruno S., a street performer and forklift operator whose last name was long concealed. He is the center of two Herzog films *The Enigma of Kaspar Hauser* and *Stroszek* (1977). The son of a prostitute, he was locked for twenty-three years in mental institutions, even though Herzog believes he was never insane.

Bruno is however very strange, bull-headed, with the simplicity and stubbornness of a child. In *Kaspar Hauser*, he looks anywhere he wants to, sometimes even craftily sideways at the camera, and then it feels not like he's looking at the audience but through us. He can possibly play no role other than himself, but that is what Herzog needs him for. On the commentary track Herzog says he was vilified in Germany for taking advantage of an unfortunate, but if you study Bruno sympathetically you may see that, by his lights, he is taking advantage of Herzog. On his commentary track, Herzog describes him as "the unknown soldier of the cinema."

Kaspar Hauser was a real historical figure who in 1828 appeared in a town square early one morning clutching the Bible and an anonymous letter. In the movie, as apparently in reality, an unknown captor kept him locked up in a cellar for about the first twenty years of his life. Adopted by the town and a friendly couple, he learns to read and write and even play the piano (in life Bruno also plays accordion and glockenspiel). Kaspar speaks as a man to whom every day is a mystery: "What are women good for?" "My coming to this world was a terribly hard fall." And think of the concept being expressed when he says, "It dreamed to me . . ."

In Herzog the line between fact and fiction is a shifting one. He cares not for accuracy but for effect, for a transcendent ecstasy. *Kaspar Hauser* tells its story not as a narrative about its hero, but as a mosaic of striking behavior and images: a line of penitents struggling up a hillside, a desert caravan led by a blind man, a stork capturing a worm. These images are unrelated to Kaspar except in the way they reflect and illuminate his struggle. The last thing Herzog is interested in is "solving" this lonely man's mystery. It is the mystery that attracts him.

All through the work of this great director, born in 1942, maker of at least fifty-four films, you can find extraordinary individuals who embody the qualities Herzog wants to evoke. In *Heart of Glass* (1976), challenged to depict a village deprived of its livelihood, he hypnotized the entire cast. In *Land of Silence and Darkness* (1971) and *Even Dwarfs Started Small* (1970), he tried to imagine the inner lives of the blind and deaf, and dwarfs. These people are not the captives of their attributes but freed by them to enter realms that are barred from us.

Herzog made two films about a German named Dieter Dengler, the documentary *Little Dieter Needs to Fly* (1997) and the fiction film *Rescue Dawn* (2006). In the first Dengler, who enlisted in the Navy, plays himself, retracing a torturous escape through the jungle from a Vietcong prison camp. In the second, he is played by Christian Bale. But Herzog has explained that he made up some of the incidents in the documentary, and the feature is in a way a documentary about the ordeal of making itself: Bale looks like a scarecrow; the real Dengler was down to eighty-five pounds. Bale's performance in a way resembles the dedication of Timothy Treadwell, the man who thought he could walk unprotected among bears in Herzog's *Grizzly Man*, a 2005 documentary based on video footage Treadwell took before finding himself mistaken. And there is Jouko Ahola, a Finnish weight lifter, twice named the world's strongest man, whom Herzog uses as the hero of *Invincible* (2001), about a Polish strong man, Jewish, who poses as an Aryan ideal in Hitler's Berlin. Not an actor, but the right person for the role.

Bale is a professional actor, yes, but hired for what he can embody, as much as for what he can do. Consider also the case of Klaus Kinski, the star of Herzog's films *Aguirre, the Wrath of God* (1972), *Fitzcarraldo* (1982), *Nosferatu* (1979), *Cobra Verde* (1987), and *Woyzeck* (1979). An actor in 135 films yes, but Kinski told me he had seen only two or three of them. A man of towering rages and terrifying rampages, which at one point allegedly had him at gunpoint with Herzog. The subject of *My Best Fiend* (1999), Herzog's savage documentary about the man he loved and reviled. To see Kinski in a Herzog film is to see a man used not as an actor, but as an instrument through which to force the film.

(141)

In some ways the most emblematic film of Herzog's career is *The Ecstasy of the Woodcarver Steiner* (1974), a documentary about a ski jumper who must start halfway down the slope, because otherwise he is too good and would fly over the landing zone and into the parking lot. His limitation is his gift, and he dreams of flying forever. So many of Herzog's protagonists, real and fictional, have such dreams of escape and are so intensely *themselves* that they carry his purpose unthinkingly.

The Enigma of Kaspar Hauser is a lyrical film about the least lyrical of men. Bruno S. has the solidity of the horses and cows he is often among, and as he confronts the world I was reminded of W. G. Sebald's remark that men and animals regard each other across a gulf of mutual incomprehension. The film's landscapes, its details from nature, its music, all embody the dream world Kaspar entered when he escaped the unchanging reality of his cellar. He never dreamed in the cellar, he explains. I think it was because he knew of nothing else than the cellar to dream about.

The film is often linked with Truffaut's *The Wild Child* (1970), set in the same century, about a boy who emerged from the forest possibly having been raised by animals. A psychologist tries to "civilize" him, but cannot change his essential nature. Kaspar is also the subject of study, and there is a professor in the film who tests Kaspar with the riddle about the two villages, one populated by those who could not tell the truth, and the other by those who could not lie. When you meet a man on a path to the two villages, Kaspar is asked, what is the one question you must ask him to determine which village he comes from? "I would ask him if he is a tree frog," Kaspar answers with some pride.

Then there is the foppish English dandy Lord Stanhope, who introduces Kaspar as his "protégé," only to find that his protégé does not like being on exhibit at fancy dress balls. Kaspar seems happy enough to allow the village to pay off its debts as an exhibit in a sideshow, however, along with a Brazilian flautist who believes that if he ever stops playing, the village will die. To prove he is Brazilian, he speaks in his own tongue, forgetting his prophecy.

The film's German title translates as, *Every Man for Himself and God Against All*. That seems to summarize Kaspar's thinking. The mystery of the captive's origins has occupied investigators ever since he first appeared. Was he the secret heir to a throne? A rich man's love child? We have glimpses of the man who held him prisoner and then set him free, standing behind him and kicking his boots to force him to walk. Who is this man? He is never explained. He may be the embodiment of Kaspar's fate. We may all have somebody behind us, kicking our boots. We are poor mortals, but it dreams to us that we can fly.

Note: Kaspar Hauser *won the Grand Jury Prize, the Critic's Prize, and the Ecumenical Prize at the 1975 Cannes Film Festival.*

Heart of Glass

MARCH 23, 2011 (RELEASED 1976)

Werner Herzog's *Heart of Glass* is a vision of man's future as desolation. In a film set entirely in a Bavarian village around 1800, it foresees the wars and calamities of the next two centuries and extends on into the twenty-first with humanity's nightfall. In the story of the failure of a small glassblowing factory, it sees the rise and collapse of the industrial revolution, the despair of communities depending on manufacture, the aimlessness of men and women without a sense of purpose.

None of these things is specifically stated. They come in the form of prophecies by a shepherd, who pronounces them in a trance to townspeople who think he must be mad. His words don't specify any of the events we know to have taken place, but they're uncanny in their ability to evoke what was coming. His words are the way a man might describe nuclear destruction, tyranny, ecological disaster, and the dominance of the crowd over the individual—if that man lacked words for the fearful images that appeared to him.

This is one of the least seen and most famous of Herzog's films, known as the one where most of the actors were hypnotized in most of the scenes. It hasn't been much seen, perhaps because it isn't to the taste of most people, seeming too slow, dark, and despairing. There's no proper story, no conclusion, and the final scene is a parable seemingly not connected to anything that has gone before. I think it should be approached like a piece of music, in which we comprehend everything in terms of mood and aura, and know how it makes us feel even if we can't say what it makes us think.

Herzog's canvas has two shots from the tops of peaks, looking down over the earth. For the rest, he sets his film entirely within the village, in a few houses, a beer hall, a glass factory, and in the surrounding forest. The people depend for their existence on the manufacture of beautiful and valued rose-colored glassware. The master glassmaker Muhlbeck has died, taking to the grave the secret of the glass. Desperate experiments are undertaken to rediscover the recipe, but all fail. A reasonable person might say, "All right then, the factory can make other kinds of glass." There are no reasonable people in the village.

Herzog indeed hypnotized them for most of the scenes; that is not simply publicity. The dialogue which they repeat under hypnosis is pronounced with a dread certainty. It lacks life and individuality. Is this how hypnotized people speak? Not necessarily. Usually they speak more like—themselves. Eerily, it occurs to me that what we may actually be hearing are the intonations of Herzog's own voice as he hypnotized them and told them what to say. He is acting through them.

He removes all individuality from the performances. He removes all self-awareness. These are not "characters," although they have distinct characteristics. They are men who have had their souls taken from them by the failure of their work. With nothing to do and nothing to hope for, they no longer have the will to survive. I am reminded of the Chinese factory workers in the documentary *Last Train Home*, who leave the provinces and live in dormitories to work for meager wages that they send home to support their children. It is a dismal life, but it is a purpose, and if while absent fifty weeks a year they lose the love of their children, then the secret of the glass has been lost.

Certain citizens stand out from the small population. There is Hias (Joseph Bierbichler), the prophetic shepherd. The heir to the factory. The dwarfish sycophant. A brazen woman. A glass blower. Two friends, who quarrel and fall drunken from a hayloft, one living, one dying because his body cushions the other's fall. The survivor dances inconsolably with his friend's body. His macabre dance, and many other scenes, take place within a beer hall where the people drink and stare.

In a well-known scene, one of the friends breaks a beer stein over the head of the other, who doesn't react. Then, slowly, he pours his own beer over the first one's head, again getting no reaction.

You can sense what Herzog is getting at. In the ordinary world one man doesn't break a mug over another's head without some ostensible reason, based on their personalities, the situation, and what they've said. All of that is redundant for Herzog's purpose. He shows the *essence* of the two men quarreling. They require no occasion. They are bereft of reason and a purpose for living, and reduced to automatons of hopelessness and hostility.

The interiors are darkly lit, with shadows gathered around them. The music of Popol Vuh seems like melodies from Purgatory. Ordinary conversation is lacking, ordinary routines abandoned. These are people solemnly waiting for . . . nothing. Although some have found the film slow and one reported dozing off, I find it terrifying in its emptiness. It is like looking down into a vertiginous fall at the edge of time. Like many good "slow" films, it seems to move more quickly on additional viewings.

I mentioned two scenes on mountain peaks. They open and close the film. The first shows a man looking down into a vast valley, through which a river of clouds pours. In 1976 these clouds were not created by CGI; Herzog used special effects to combine the man and the image. I learned he worked twelve days to get the shot. The effect is haunting. What it evokes for me is the sense of Man standing above Time and glimpsing it on its flow toward Eternity. I learn from the critic Neil Young that Herzog's "debt to 19th-century German artists is evident, with Caspar David Friedrich prominent among the influences." He says this shot "recreates his famous 'Wanderer Over a Sea of Fog.'"

The final scene involves a man on a mountain peak who looks out to sea. Herzog intercuts sea birds on the mountain side, moving in nervous waves of flight. A narrator explains that the man concludes there must be something on the other side of the ocean. Transfixed by his conviction, men set out to cross the sea, rowing with fierce determination in a pitifully small boat after land disappears behind them and no land appears before them. The narrator tells us they took it as a good omen that the birds followed them out to sea.

What does this mean? It is better to row into oblivion than to wait for it to come to you? I don't know. Some images are complete without translation into words. *Heart of Glass* strikes me as a film of such images. From it I get a feeling that evokes my gloom as I see a world sinking into self-destruction, and feel I am lucky to be old because there may not be another lifetime's length of happiness left for most people on this planet. For most of my time here there was still rose-colored glass.

Herzog fascinates me. I feel a film like *Heart of Glass* comes as close to any single one of his titles to expressing the inchoate feelings in his heart. He was once asked what he would do if he had one day to live. It's a meaningless question, but I appreciated his answer: "Martin Luther said that if he knew the world were ending tomorrow, he would plant a tree. I would start a new film."

Stroszek

JULY 7, 2002 (RELEASED 1977)

Who else but Werner Herzog would make a film about a retarded ex-prisoner, a little old man, and a prostitute, who leave Germany to begin a new life in a house trailer in Wisconsin? Who else would shoot the film in the hometown of Ed Gein, the murderer who inspired *Psycho?* Who else would cast all the local roles with locals? Who else would end the movie with a policeman radioing, "We've got a truck on fire, can't find the switch to turn the ski lift off, and can't stop the dancing chicken. Send an electrician."

Stroszek is one of the oddest films ever made. It is impossible for the audience to anticipate a single shot or development. We watch with a kind of fascination, because Herzog cuts loose from narrative and follows his characters through the relentless logic of their adventure. Then there is the haunting impact of the performance by Bruno S., who is at every moment playing himself.

The personal history of Bruno S. forms the psychic background for the film. Bruno was the son of a prostitute, beaten so badly he was deaf for a time. He was in a mental institution from the ages of three to twenty-six—and yet was not, in Herzog's opinion, mentally ill; it was more that the blows and indifference of life had shaped him into a man of intense concentration, tunnel vision, and narrow social skills. He looks as if he has long been expecting the worst to happen.

Herzog, who with Wim Wenders and Rainer Werner Fassbinder brought forth the New German Cinema in the late 1960s and 1970s, saw Bruno in a documentary about street musicians. He cast him in the extraordinary film *Every Man for Himself and God Against All* (1974), also known as *The Enigma of Kaspar Hauser*. It told the story of an eighteenth century man locked in a cellar until he was an adult, and then set loose on the streets to make what sense he could of the world. Bruno was uncannily right for the role, and right, too, for *Stroszek*, which Herzog wrote in four days.

Ah, but there is a reason why the screenplay came quickly. Herzog had the location already in mind. He and the American documentarian Errol Morris had become fascinated by the story of Ed Gein, who dug up all of the corpses in a circle around his mother's grave. Did he also dig up his mother? They decided they had to open the grave to see for themselves. In Q&As we had during tributes at Facets in Chicago and the Walker Art Center in Minneapolis, Herzog told me the story: Morris did not turn up as scheduled in Plainfield, Wisconsin, the grave was never opened, but Herzog's car broke down there and he met the mechanic whose shop provides a key location and character for the film.

With the destination in mind, Herzog found the story writing itself. The film opens with Bruno (Bruno S.) being released from prison, walking into a bar, and meeting Eva (Eva Mattes), a prostitute whose pimp mistreats her. He offers her refuge in his apartment, which has been looked after by the elderly, tiny Mr. Scheitz (Clemens Scheitz). Mr. Scheitz announces that his nephew in Railroad Flats, Wisconsin, has invited him to move there. It is time, Bruno announces, for them all to begin their new lives. Eva raises money through prostitution (her clients are Turkish workers at a construction site), and the three find themselves in Wisconsin and in possession of a magnificent new forty-foot 1973 Fleetwood mobile home.

But this plot summary sounds mundane, and the tone of the movie is so strange. *Stroszek* is not a comedy, but I don't know how to describe it. Perhaps as a peculiarity. We get the sense that Herzog is adding detail on the spot: as Railroad Flats happens to the characters, it happens to the film. Mr. Scheitz's nephew is played by Clayton Szalpinski, the very mechanic who repaired Herzog's car, and he regales the newcomers with local color. A farmer and his enormous tractor have gone missing, and Clayton believes they are to be found at the bottom of one of the many local lakes. He has a metal detector, and on days when the ice is thick enough, he searches.

Bruno is sure the idyll cannot last. He is positive that the papers they signed at the bank will sooner or later require them to make payments, and he is right. Scott McKain plays a painfully polite bank employee who tries to explain that the TV set "might/would" have to be repossessed (he often uses two words to take the edge off of both; McKain perfectly captures the tone of a man embarrassed to be bringing up money). Eventually there is the unforgettable sight of the Fleetwood being towed off the land, leaving Bruno to stare at the forbidding winter Wisconsin landscape. He knew something like this would happen.

The thing about most American movies is that the actors in them look like the kinds of people who might be hired for a movie. They don't have to be handsome, but they have to be presentable — to fall within a certain range. If they are too strange, how can they find steady work? Herzog often frees himself of this restraint by using non-actors. Clayton Szalpinski, for example, has an overbite and backwoods speech patterns, but he is right for his role, and no professional actor could play a small-town garage mechanic any better. And Bruno S. is a phenomenon. Herzog says that sometimes, to get in the mood for a scene, Bruno would scream for an hour or two. In his acting he always seems to be totally present: there is nothing held back, no part of his mind elsewhere. He projects a kind of sincerity that is almost disturbing, and you realize that there is no corner anywhere within Bruno for a lie to take hold.

Many movies end with hopeless characters turning to crime. No movie ends like *Stroszek*. Bruno and Mr. Scheitz take a rifle and go to rob the bank, which is closed, so they rob the barber shop next door of thirty-two dollars and, leaving their car running, walk directly across the street to a supermarket, where Bruno has time to pick up a frozen turkey before the cops arrest Mr. Scheitz. Bruno then drives to a nearby amusement arcade, where he feeds in quarters to make

(149)

chickens dance and play the piano. Then he boards a ski lift to go around and around and around.

This last sequence is just about the best he has ever filmed, Herzog says on the commentary track of the DVD. His crew members hated the dancing chicken so much they refused to participate, and he shot the footage himself. The chicken is a "great metaphor," he says—for what, he's not sure. My theory: a force we cannot comprehend puts some money in the slot, and we dance until the money runs out.

Stroszek has been reviewed as an attack on American society, but actually German society comes out looking worse, and all of the Americans seem naive, simple and nice, even the bank official. The film's tragedy unfolds because these three people have nothing in common and no reason to think they can live together in Wisconsin or anywhere else. For a time Eva sleeps with Bruno, but then she closes her door to him, and in a remarkable scene he shows her a twisted sculpture and says, using the third person, "This is a schematic model of how it looks inside Bruno. They're closing all the doors on him."

Earlier in the film, in Berlin, after he loses his job and his girl, Bruno goes to a doctor for help. This man (Vaclav Vojta) listens carefully, is sympathetic, has no answers, and takes Bruno into a ward where premature babies are being tended. Look, he says, how tenacious the grip reflex is, even in this little infant. A child clings to the doctor's big fingers. Bruno looks. We can never tell from his face what he is thinking. The baby cries, and the doctor tenderly cradles it, kissing its ear, and it goes to sleep. That is, perhaps, what Bruno needs.

Nosferatu the Vampyre

NOVEMBER 24, 2011 (RELEASED 1979)

There is a quality to the color photography in Werner Herzog's *Nosferatu the Vampyre* that seeps into your bones. It would be inadequate to call it "saturated." It is rich, heavy, deep. The earth looks cold and dirty. There isn't a lot of green, and it looks wet. Mountains look craggy, gray, sharp-edged. Interiors are filmed in bold reds and browns and whites—whites, especially, for the faces, and above all for Count Dracula's. It is a film of remarkable beauty but makes no effort to attract or visually coddle us. The spectacular journey by foot and coach to Dracula's remote Transylvanian castle is deliberately not made to seem scenic.

There is often something fearful and awesome in Herzog's depiction of nature. It is not uplifting so much as remorseless. Clouds fall low and drift like water. Peaks tower in intimidation. Shadows hint at horrors. The simple peasants that Jonathan Harker encounters on his journey are not colorful and friendly, but withdraw from him. Herzog takes his time before allowing us our first sight of Dracula; his stage has been set by words and the looks in eyes of people who cannot believe he is seeking the Count.

Herzog follows the structure of F. W. Murnau's famous *Nosferatu* (1922), one of the greatest of all silent films. That was based on Bram Stoker's 1897 novel *Dracula*. Murnau changed the character names for copyright reasons, and Herzog was free to use the originals: Dracula (Klaus Kinski), the land agent Jonathan Harker (Bruno Ganz), his wife

Lucy (Isabelle Adjani), Dr. Van Helsing (Walter Ladengast), and he of the maniacal laugh, Renfield (Roland Topor).

The film opens with Renfield offering Harker a large commission to travel to Dracula's castle and sell him an isolated property in town. Harker wants the money because he thinks his wife deserves a nicer house. Renfield's spasmodic laughter doesn't deter him. His journey takes a great deal more time than in the many other movies based on this famous story. There is an ominous scene at an inn where he mentions Dracula's name and the entire room falls silent, simply staring at him. Herzog takes his time building up anticipation before Dracula's entrance.

No coach will take Harker to the castle. No one will sell or rent him a horse. Renfield continues on foot, walking narrow pathways above cruel chasms. Finally Dracula's coach comes out to fetch him. It looks like (because it is) a hearse. The door to the castle creaks open and we regard Dracula. In creating the vampire, Herzog follows the striking art direction of the Murnau film, making the count look more like an animal than a human being. None of your handsome, sleek vampires played by Tom Cruise. The head is shaved. The face and skull are clown white. The fingernails are spears. The ears are pointed like a bat's. The eyes are sunken and rimmed in black and red. Most extraordinary of all are the two prominent fangs in the center of the mouth, placed like a bat's, unconcealed. In most movies Dracula's teeth are up and to the sides, more easily concealed. Here there can be no mistaking them.

Many famous details are paid homage. The line, "Listen. The children of the night make their music." The Count's barely controlled lust when Harker cuts his thumb with a bread knife. The meals mysteriously appearing without servants. Then the race as Dracula goes by sea and Harker by land to the city of Bremen, where Lucy is in danger.

Herzog is the most original of filmmakers, not much given to remakes. His only other one, *The Bad Lieutenant: Port of Call New Orleans* (2009), was so different from the original that only the idea of a corrupt cop was kept. Why was he drawn to remake one of the most famous and least dated of German silent films?

I think it was partly because of love — for Murnau, and for the film, which suits the macabre strain in some of his own work. It was partly in homage. And I suspect it was above all because he had the resource of Klaus Kinski. He had first laid eyes on Kinski when he was still a boy, and the fierce-eyed actor lived in the same building. "I knew at that moment," he told me, "that it was my destiny to make films, and direct Kinski in them." The two developed an almost symbiotic relationship, which led at times to death threats against each other, and also to such extraordinary work as *Aguirre, the Wrath of God* and *Fitzcarraldo*. Kinski of all actors could most easily create the driven and the mad.

To say of someone that they were born to play a vampire is a strange compliment, but if you will compare the two versions of Nosferatu you might agree with me that only Kinski could have equaled or rivaled Max Schreck's performance. Opposite him Herzog cast Isabelle Adjani, a French beauty who is used here not only for her facial perfection but for her curious quality of seeming to exist on an ethereal plane. Adjani does not easily play ordinary women. Her skin always seems unusually white and smooth, as is porcelain. Here she provides a pure object for Dracula's fangs.

The other masterstroke of casting is Roland Topor, as the Bremen realtor. Topor did a fair amount of acting but was principally an author and artist, the cofounder of the Panic Movement with Alejandro Jodorowsky (*El Topo*). Herzog recalls watching a trivial German TV show on which Topor's weird high-pitched giggle seemed to evoke perfect madness. Here it is used to suggest the unwholesome nature of his relationship with Dracula.

Nosferatu the Vampyre cannot be confined to the category of "horror film." It is about dread itself, and how easily the unwary can fall into evil. Bruno Ganz makes an ideal Harker because he sidesteps any temptation to play a hero and plays a devoted husband who naively dismisses alarming warnings. He is loving, then resolute, then uncertain, then fearful, then desperate, and finally mad—lost.

Although I don't believe *Nosferatu* had a particularly large budget, its historical detail looks unfaked and convincing. Herzog travels much in search of arresting imagery; the mummies at the start are from Mexico, the mountains are the Carpathian, the castles and castle ruins are in the Czech Republic, Slovakia, and Germany, and I believe the city with canals is in the Netherlands.

That said, Herzog told me that some shots were set up to use the same locations that Murnau used, and often had similar compositions. Once I asked him why he took a crew far into the South American rain forests to shoot *Aguirre* and *Fitzcarraldo*, and he said he believed in "the voodoo of locations." A rain forest forty miles away from a city would have *felt* wrong. The actors would project a different energy if they knew they truly were buried in a wilderness. We would be able to sense it. In the same spirit, I suppose, Kinski standing where Murnau's actor Max Schreck stood would generate an energy. This film is haunted by the earlier one.

I wonder if Kinski himself believed this was a role he was born to play. Famously temperamental, his emotions on a hair trigger, he endured four hours of makeup daily without complaining. The bat ears had to be destroyed in removal, and constructed again every morning. It's as if he regarded Schreck's performance and wanted to step in and claim the character as partly his own.

One striking quality of the film is its beauty. Herzog's pictorial eye is not often enough credited. His films always upstage it with their themes. We are focused on what happens, and there are few "beauty shots." Look here at his control of the color palate, his off-center compositions, of the dramatic counterpoint of light and dark. Here is a film that does honor to the seriousness of vampires. No, I don't believe in them. But if they were real, here is how they must look.

Fitzcarraldo

AUGUST 28, 2005 (RELEASED 1982)

Werner Herzog's *Fitzcarraldo* is one of the great visions of the cinema, and one of the great follies. One would not have been possible without the other. This is a movie about an opera-loving madman who is determined to drag a boat overland from one river system to another. In making the film, Herzog was determined to actually do that, which is more than can be said for Brian Sweeney Fitzgerald, the Irishman whose story inspired him.

Fitzcarraldo is one of those brave and epic films, like *Apocalypse Now* or *2001*, where we are always aware both of the film and of the making of the film. Herzog could have used special effects for his scenes of the 360-ton boat being hauled up a muddy forty-degree slope in the jungle, but he believed we could tell the difference: "This is not a plastic boat." Watching the film, watching Fitzcarraldo (Klaus Kinski) raving in the jungle in his white suit and floppy panama hat, watching Indians operating a block-and-tackle system to drag the boat out of the muck, we're struck by the fact that this is actually happening, that this huge boat is inching its way onto land—as Fitzcarraldo (who got his name because the locals could not pronounce "Fitzgerald") serenades the jungle with his scratchy old Caruso recordings.

The story of the making of *Fitzcarraldo* is told in *Burden of Dreams* (1982), a documentary by Les Blank and Maureen Gosling, who spent time in the jungle with Herzog, his mutinous crew, and his eccentric star. After you see the Herzog film and *Burden*, it's clear that everyone associated with the film was marked, or scarred, by the experience; there is an impassioned speech in *Burden* where Herzog denounces the jungle as "vile and base" and says, "It's a land which God, if he exists, has created in anger."

Fitzcarraldo opens on the note of madness, which it will sustain. Out of the dark void of the Amazon comes a boat, its motor dead, the shock-haired Kinski furiously rowing at the prow, while his mistress (Claudia Cardinale) watches anxiously behind him. They are late for the opera. He has made some money with an ice-making machine, she is a madam whose bordello services wealthy rubber traders, and as they talk their way into an opera house, Fitzcarraldo knows his mission in life: he will become rich, build an opera house in the jungle, and hire Caruso to sing in it.

Fortunes in this district are built on rubber. He obtains the rights to four hundred square miles that are thought to be useless because a deadly rapids prevents a boat from reaching them. But if he could bring a boat from another river, his dream could come true. The real Fitzgerald only moved a thirty-two-ton boat between rivers, and he disassembled it first. Hearing the story, Herzog was struck by the image of a boat moving up a hillside, and the rest of the screenplay followed.

His production can be described as a series of emergencies. A border war between Peru and Ecuador prevented him from using his first location. He found another location and shot for four months with Jason Robards playing Fitzcarraldo and Mick Jagger playing his loony sidekick. Then Robards contracted amoebic dysentery and flew home, forbidden by his doctors to return, and Jagger dropped out. Herzog turned to Klaus Kinski, the legendary wild man who had starred in his *Aguirre, the Wrath of God* (1972) and *Nosferatu* (1979). Kinski was a better choice for the role than Robards, for the same reason a real boat was better than a model: Robards would have been playing a madman, but to see Kinski is to be convinced of his ruling angers and demons.

Herzog has always been more fascinated by image than story, and here he sears his images into the film. He worked with indigenous Amazonian Indians, whose faces become one of the important elements of the work. An early scene shows Fitzcarraldo awakened from sleep to find his bed surrounded by children. There is a scene where Indians gaze impassively at the river, not even noticing Fitzcarraldo as he ranges up and down their line, peering wildly into their faces. There is another scene where he and his boat crew eat dinner while Indians crowd into the mess room and stare at them. And scenes simply of faces, watchful, judgmental, trying to divine what drives the man in the white suit.

Herzog admitted that he could have filmed his entire production a day or two outside Quito, the capital of Ecuador. Instead, he filmed in the rain forest, five hundred miles from the nearest sizable city. That allows shots like the one where Fitzcarraldo and his boat captain stand in a platform at the top of the tallest tree, surveying the vastness around them. He has spoken of the "voodoo of location," which caused him to shoot part of his *Nosferatu* in the same places where Murnau filmed his 1926 silent version. He felt the jungle location would "bring out special qualities in the actors and even the crew." This was more true than he could have suspected, and in the fourth year of his struggle to make the film, exhausted, he said, "I am running out of fantasy. I don't know what else can happen now. Even if I get that boat over the mountain, nobody on this earth will convince me to be happy about that, not until the end of my days."

(157)

Burden of Dreams tells of arrows shot from the forest, of the boat slipping back down the hill, of the Brazilian engineer resigning and walking away after telling Herzog there was a 70 percent chance that the cables would snap and dozens of lives would be lost. On a commentary track, we learn more horrifying details; a crew member, bitten by a deadly snake, saved his own life by instantly cutting off his foot with the chain saw he was holding. In an outtake from *Burden*, which Herzog used in *My Best Fiend* (1999), his documentary about his stormy relationship with Kinski, we see the actor raging crazily on the set. *Burden* has an image that will do for the entire production: Herzog wading through mud up to his knees, pulling free each leg to take another step.

The movie is imperfect, but transcendent; this story could not have been filmed on this location in this way and been perfect without being less of a film. The conclusion, the scene with the cigar, for example, is an anticlimax; but then everything must be an anticlimax after the boat goes up the hill. What is crucial is that Herzog does not hurry his story along; he seeks not the progress of the plot, but the resonance of the images. Consider a sequence where the boat actually bangs and crashes its way through the deadly Pongo das Mortes, the Rapids of Death. Another director might have made this a routine action scene, with quick cuts and lots of noise; Herzog makes it a slow and frightful procession down real currents in a real ship, with a phonograph playing Caruso until the needle is knocked loose. It looks more horrifying to see the huge ship slowly floating to its destiny.

Among directors of the last four decades, has anyone created a more impassioned and adventurous career than Werner Herzog? Most people have only seen a few of his films, or none; he cannot be fully appreciated without a familiarity with his many documentaries and more obscure features (such as *Heart of Glass* and *Stroszek*). His 2005 documentary *Grizzly Man*, about a man who spent thirteen summers with the grizzly bears of Alaska, is the spiritual brother of *Fitzcarraldo* — both times, men are driven by obsession to challenge the wilderness. Again and again, in films shot in Africa, Australia, Southeast Asia, and South America, he has been drawn to the farthest reaches of the earth and to the people who live there with their images uncorrupted by the thin gruel of mass media.

"I don't want to live in a world without lions, and without people who are lions," he says in *Burden of Dreams*. At the darkest hour in *Fitzcarraldo*, when Robards fell sick and he had to abandon four months of shooting, Herzog returned to get more backing from investors. They had heard he was finding it impossible to get the ship up the mountain and asked if it would not be wiser to take his losses and quit. His reply: "How can you ask this question? If I abandon this project, I will be a man without dreams, and I don't want to live like that. I live my life or I end my life with this project." With Herzog, that has often been the case.

Part 5 〉 Summing Up

A Letter to Werner Herzog

IN PRAISE OF RAPTUROUS TRUTH

NOVEMBER 17, 2007

Dear Werner,

You have done me the astonishing honor of dedicating your
new film, *Encounters at the End of the World*, to me. Since I have
admired your work beyond measure for the almost forty years
since we first met, I do not need to explain how much this
kindness means to me. When I saw the film at the Toronto
Film Festival and wrote to thank you, I said I wondered if it
would be a conflict of interest for me to review the film, even
though of course you have made a film I could not possibly
dislike. I said I thought perhaps the solution was to simply
write you a letter.

But I will review the film, my friend, when it arrives in
theaters on its way to airing on the Discovery Channel. I will
review it, and I will challenge anyone to describe my praise as
inaccurate.

I will review it because I love great films and must share my
enthusiasm.

This is not that review. It is the letter. It is a letter to a man
whose life and career have embodied a vision of the cinema
that challenges moviegoers to ask themselves questions not
only about films but about lives. About their lives, and the
lives of the people in your films, and your own life.

Without ever making a movie for solely commercial

PART 5: SUMMING UP

reasons, without ever having a dependable source of financing, without the attention of the studios and the oligarchies that decide what may be filmed and shown, you have directed at least fifty-five films or television productions, and we will not count the operas. You have worked all the time, because you have depended on your imagination instead of budgets, stars, or publicity campaigns. You have had the visions and made the films and trusted people to find them, and they have. It is safe to say you are as admired and venerated as any filmmaker alive—among those who have heard of you, of course. Those who do not know your work, and the work of your comrades in the independent film world, are missing experiences that might shake and inspire them.

I have not seen all your films, and do not have a perfect memory, but I believe you have never made a film depending on sex, violence, or chase scenes. Oh, there is violence in *Lessons of Darkness*, about the Kuwait oil fields aflame, or *Grizzly Man*, or *Rescue Dawn*. But not "entertaining violence." There is sort of a chase scene in *Even Dwarfs Started Small*. But there aren't any romances.

You have avoided this content, I suspect, because it lends itself so seductively to formulas, and you want every film to be absolutely original.

You have also avoided all "obligatory scenes," including artificial happy endings. And special effects (everyone knows about the real boat in *Fitzcarraldo*, but even the swarms of rats in *Nosferatu* are real rats, and your strong man in *Invincible* actually lifted the weights). And you don't use musical scores that tell us how to feel about the content. Instead, you prefer freestanding music that evokes a mood: you use classical music, opera, oratorios, requiems, aboriginal music, the sounds of the sea, bird cries, and of course Popol Vuh.

All of these decisions proceed from your belief that the audience must be able to believe what it sees. Not its "truth," but its actuality, its ecstatic truth.

You often say this modern world is starving for images. That the media pound the same paltry ideas into our heads time and again, and that we need to see around the edges or over the top. When you open *Encounters at the End of the World* by following a marine biologist under the ice floes of the South Pole, and listening to the alien sounds of the creatures who thrive there, you show me a place on my planet I did not know about, and I am richer. You are the most curious of men. You are like the storytellers of old, returning from far lands with spellbinding tales.

I remember at the Telluride Film Festival, ten or twelve years ago, when you told me you had a video of your latest documentary. We found a TV set in a hotel room and I saw *Bells from the Deep*, a film in which you wandered through Russia observing strange beliefs.

There were the people who lived near a deep lake, and believed that on its bottom there was a city populated by angels. To see it, they had to wait until winter when the water was crystal clear, and then creep spread-eagled onto the ice. If the ice was too thick, they could not see well enough. Too thin, and they might drown. We heard the ice creaking beneath them as they peered for their vision.

Then we met a monk who looked like Rasputin. You found that there were hundreds of "Rasputins," some claiming to be Jesus Christ, walking through Russia with their prophecies and warnings. These people, and their intense focus, and the music evoking another world (as your sound tracks always do) held me in their spell, and we talked for some time about the film, and then you said, "But you know, Roger, it is all made up." I did not understand. "It is not real. I invented it."

I didn't know whether to believe you about your own film. But I know you speak of "ecstatic truth," of a truth beyond the merely factual, a truth that records not the real world but the world as we dream it.

Your documentary *Little Dieter Needs to Fly* begins with a

real man, Dieter Dengler, who really was a prisoner of the
Vietcong, and who really did escape through the jungle and
was the only American who freed himself from a Vietcong
prison camp. As the film opens, we see him entering his house,
and compulsively opening and closing windows and doors, to
be sure he is not locked in. "That was my idea," you told me.
"Dieter does not really do that. But it is how he feels."

The line between truth and fiction is a mirage in your work.

Some of the documentaries contain fiction, and some of
the fiction films contain fact. Yes, you really did haul a boat up
a mountainside in *Fitzcarraldo*, even though any other director
would have used a model, or special effects. You organized the
ropes and pulleys and workers in the middle of the Amazonian
rain forest, and hauled the boat up into the jungle. And later,
when the boat seemed to be caught in a rapids that threatened
its destruction, it really was. This in a fiction film. The
audience will know if the shots are real, you said, and that will
affect how they see the film.

I understand this. What must be true, must be true. What
must not be true, can be made more true by invention. Your
films, frame by frame, contain a kind of rapturous truth that
transcends the factually mundane. And yet when you find
something real, you show it.

You based *Grizzly Man* on the videos that Timothy
Treadwell took in Alaska during his summers with wild bears.
In Antarctica, in *Encounters at the End of the World*, you talk
with real people who have chosen to make their lives there
in a research station. Some are "linguists on a continent
with no language," you note, others are "PhDs working as
cooks." When a marine biologist cuts a hole in the ice and
dives beneath it, he does not use a rope to find his way back
to the small escape circle in the limitless shelf above him,
because it would restrict his research. When he comes up, he
simply hopes he can find the hole. This is all true, but it is also
ecstatic truth.

In the process of compiling your life's work, you have never lost your sense of humor. Your narrations are central to the appeal of your documentaries, and your wonder at human nature is central to your fiction. In one scene you can foresee the end of life on earth, and in another show us country musicians picking their guitars and banjos on the roof of a hut at the South Pole. You did not go to Antarctica, you assure us at the outset, to film cute penguins. But you did film one cute penguin, a penguin that was disoriented, and was steadfastly walking in precisely the wrong direction—into an ice vastness the size of Texas. "And if you turn him around in the right direction," you say, "he will turn himself around, and keep going in the wrong direction, until he starves and dies." The sight of that penguin waddling optimistically toward his doom would be heartbreaking, except that he is so sure he is correct.

(165)

But I have started to wander off like the penguin, my friend.

I have started out to praise your work, and have ended by describing it. Maybe it is the same thing. You and your work are unique and invaluable, and you ennoble the cinema when so many debase it. You have the audacity to believe that if you make a film about anything that interests you, it will interest us as well. And you have proven it.

With admiration,
Roger

Herzog and the Forms of Madness

JULY 20, 2008

I had in mind to write about something else this week, but our new software platform for the blog was acting up (as you might have noticed), and in the meantime I received an intriguing communication from a reader, the art critic Daniel Quiles, about Werner Herzog. Yes, there has been a lot about Herzog on the site recently, but in my mind there can never be too much. He and a few other directors keep the movies vibrating for me. Not every movie needs to vibrate, but unless a few do, the thrill is gone.

Herzog seems to react strongly to subjects he wants to make a film about. You never hear him saying someone "brought me a project," or his agent sent him a screenplay. Every one of his films is in some sense autobiographical: it is about what consumed him at that moment. The form of the film might be fiction, might be fact, might be a hybrid. The material dictates the form, and often his presence in the film dictates the material: it would not exist if he were not there. In a way, that's what Quiles is writing about in connection with *Encounters at the End of the World*.

Quiles: First of all, no other director in history could turn a blizzard-safety exercise into an allegory for the extinction of human life on this planet. This is sheer mastery of the documentary form.

Two additional issues that interest me are the motif of language and Herzog's occasionally dismissive treatment of the dayworkers at McMurdo. Apocalyptic as the film is, it is in equal measure profoundly optimistic about the myriad languages that persist even in Antarctica, both human and animal. While the scientific languages we encounter have to be translated for us to comprehend them, Herzog does his best to do justice to their different modes of understanding the universe and bringing it "into its magnificence," as the Bulgarian tractor driver concludes the film. Language—what facilitates any "encounter" and puts the non-sense of the universe into sense—is the life force that struggles against our ongoing demise.

Hence Herzog's outrage at the lapsed linguist who professes not to care that a language has died (though it obliterated his career and sent him to the middle of nowhere, so perhaps he did). Here, in a brief sequence, the film gets quite un-Herzogian. This man is one of two characters whom the director does not allow to speak for themselves, using an interesting and hilarious trick of cutting them off via voice-over. To me this runs contradictory to Herzog's recent films, in which Treadwellesque characters are given center stage and allowed to run their mouths to their hearts' content. In *Encounters*, it is the highly skilled masters of their languages (the scientists) who are idealized, while the professional adventurers of McMurdo, who labor in miserable conditions at high salaries to fund globetrotting excursions for the rest of the year, are bores and phonies, akin to the buffoon running around the world breaking Guinness Book records.

(167)

Remarkably, Herzog laments that adventure ended more than a century ago; these people never got the memo. Treadwell of *Grizzly Man* didn't get it, either, but he was mad enough to put himself in harm's way and film it (not unlike our dear director). Treadwell and Graham Dorrington in *The White Diamond* seem like two poles for Herzog now, mad outcast and mad scientist, with those in between them not proving interesting enough. In *Encounters*, I get the sense that Herzog, like the old master that he is, is favoring the Dorrington side, that of the scientist, that of craft and virtuosity.

Ebert again. Quiles is right that Herzog has no interest in the in-between. Whether "mad outcast and mad scientist" represent the two poles of his work is open to question for this reason: are they mad? Bruno S. of *Kaspar Hauser* and *Stroszek* was apparently in some degree mentally ill, or damaged as a child. Klaus Kinski behaved insanely at times, but I sense he was crafty like a fox, using his reputation to get his way. It wasn't a stretch for him to play the title role in *Nosferatu the Vampyre*. But for the most part Herzog deals with sane people at the extremes. They can think logically, and he is fascinated by the choices their logical thinking has driven them to.

Quiles cites *The White Diamond*, the film about a man who designed an airship to investigate the unknown ecosystem that lives in the treetops of the Amazon and has no contact with the ground. When you see Dorrington's teardrop airship and learn of its safety history, you may put him among the outcasts, but when he talks of uncounted species never seen by man, you can return him to the scientists. And what of Herzog himself? On the airship's maiden flight, he insists on handling the camera himself, because (1) he does not want to risk the life of his cinematographer, and (2) if there is only one flight, how else to obtain the footage? What is he here? Mad artist?

Not mad at all. Simply brave, and like all great directors, determined to get that footage. If the airship crashes, there may be no more Herzog but if he doesn't go, there will be no film. There is also a Herzog movie, *Lessons of Darkness*, in which he put himself in the middle of the blazing oil wells of Kuwait. And one, shown at Telluride but not I believe widely released, in which he and his team were trapped on a mountaintop by a blizzard and nearly died. He grows a little annoyed as people cite some of these stories, because they make him seem reckless, and that he is not. He does what he must to get his film, calculating the situation, hoping not to be surprised.

He is annoyed when some writers (including me) have suggested he went hundreds of miles up the Amazon on a lark, seeking the "voodoo of location" for *Fitzcarraldo*. In fact, as he corrected me, he had a perfectly sensible location, but it was burnt down in a border war, and he was forced to move to the only other place where two tributaries of the Amazon were close enough to pull a boat overland between them. (His determination to physically move a real boat raises other questions, but never mind.)

The phrase "voodoo of location" was first used by Herzog in my hearing when he explained that, for his *Nosferatu*, he sought out and used as many of the same locations as he could from the silent classic by Murnau. In some sense the genius of Murnau would haunt the film. If I were a producer asked to finance the film, that would sound like madness, but as a film critic, it makes perfect sense to me.

Comment by Werner Herzog

JULY 21, 2008

The producer of *Grizzly Man* and *Encounters*, Erik Nelson, forwarded me your conversation with an art critic (Quiles), and I have the feeling that these people do not have the ability to simply look straight at a movie any more.

If you find it useful, please introduce my remarks into this ongoing discourse (without giving my e-mail address away).

About the linguist: I intentionally steered the discourse with him into the terrain of dying languages. Both of us are deeply worried by the prospect of the future: about 90 percent of all of the roughly 6,500 spoken languages today will be extinct well before the end of this century. I am already in the planning stage to do a long-term documentary project on last speakers of a language.

It is a total misreading of the sequence that Bill Jirsa (the linguist) does not care that possibly during our conversation a language had died.

I had to cut him off and summarize his travails with academia, as this was a highly complex story which went on and on for about forty minutes. The next following sequence with the computer expert and traveler Karen Joyce I had to cut short as well, and give only some taste of her way of exploring the world, as she went on nonstop for about two hours—without ever making a full stop or a comma in her tales. There was literally no chance during editing to ever get out of her most wonderful stories. I love both of them dearly, and they have forgiven me that my film's total running time had to be under two hours.

No one is a phony in my film. They are most fascinating human beings, and I wish I could have them as friends forever, even though our encounters were so brief.

The pogo-stick man breaking Guinness book records was archival footage I found. I never met him, but his story and attitude make a clear point.

Comment by Daniel Quiles

JULY 21, 2008

I am honored to be brought into dialogue with not just one but two of my models, especially about a movie that I adored as much as *Encounters*.

I hope to clarify two of my points, as briefly as I can.

First, I would soften my language with regard to the dayworkers at McMurdo. Indeed, in the film there are only two instances of the voice-over interruption that I mention above, and the other such workers at the station are treated as eloquent and essential voices. So I apologize if I suggested that Herzog sets up a simplistic dichotomy between the workers and the scientists; this is not the case.

My interest was in the film's contention that "adventure" died more than a century ago, and the implications of this idea for the mythmaking around Herzog's work on the one hand (*Fitzcarraldo* and co.), and for the subjects of recent documentaries such as *Grizzly Man* and *The White Diamond* on the other. If the category of "adventure," tied as it was to the notion of the frontier, is over, what does it mean to pursue extremes in remote locations? I don't have an answer, though I was venturing that maybe it could be tied to language—to making sense of the world.

Second, in response to Roger: my use of the term "mad" was a bit careless. I would be the last person to suggest that Kinski, Treadwell, or Dorrington were in any way "insane." One thing that I value in Herzog's films is how they obliterate the categories of "normal" and "abnormal," most poignantly in the Bruno S. films. Kaspar Hauser, for example, has more insight into the culture in which he lives than anyone else. Dorrington's risk-taking ultimately pays off with unprecedented discoveries.

I guess the idea that comes up again and again here is "extremes."

Extremes are relative, of course. Some of the best humor in *Encounters* comes from the matter-of-factness of so much of the activity there; for these people, this is normal life.

As for not being able to "look straight" at a movie, I suppose I can only plead that while I watch a film, I look very straight indeed. Once the film is over, however, I think about it, and patterns occur to me. I like to think that my thoughts are part of the world of the film, insofar as I am part of its audience.

Additional Comment by Daniel Quiles

OCTOBER 24, 2016

My original text was included in a personal e-mail to Roger and was never intended for online publication as it was written — let alone for Werner Herzog to see! At that time, Roger was communicating freely with a variety of admirers and routinely posting their comments and e-mails to his blog. As is clear in my follow-up comments, I was dismayed to have in any way offended a director whose work I admire greatly. My e-mail had never been intended as a criticism of *Encounters*, but rather as a thinking-through of its possible relationships to Herzog's other films. My effusive and wordy prose is evidence of a critical voice then still in formation, and of an exhilaration that came from direct access to Roger. This unexpected exchange should stand as a tribute to his remarkable generosity toward his readers in the final decade of his life; he actively encouraged and supported our own writing.

The Great Ecstasy of the Sculptor Herzog

JANUARY 26, 2013

A man said to the universe
"Sir, I exist!"
"However," replied the universe,
"The fact has not created in me
A sense of obligation."
— Stephen Crane

That man can be found at the center of Werner Herzog's films. He is Aguirre. He is Fitzcarraldo. He is the Nosferatu. He is Timothy Treadwell, who lived among the grizzlies. He is little Dieter Dengler, who needed to fly. She is Fini Straubinger, who lived in a land of silence and darkness since she was twelve. He is Kaspar Hauser. He is Klaus Kinski. He is the man who will not leave the slopes of the Guadeloupe volcano when it is about to explode. He is those who live in the Antarctic. She is Juliana Koepcke, whose plane crashed in the rain forest and she walked out alive. He is Graham Dorrington, who flew one of the smallest airships ever built to study the life existing only in the treetops of that rain forest.

He is the sculptor Steiner, a ski jumper who learned to fly so far the landing slopes could not contain him. He is the man or woman who left his handprint on the wall of the Chauvet Cave thirty-two thousand years ago. He is Michael Perry, with days to go on death row. He is Woyzeck, who submitted without complaint to the medical experiments ordered by the German army. He is Dr. Gene Scott, who preached his gospel for long unbroken hours on cable TV, while seated wearing strange hats and smoking cigars. He is Hias, the man who stands on a mountaintop engulfed in tumbling clouds. He is the bad lieutenant. He is Herschel Steinschneider, the Jewish strongman in Nazi Germany. He is the alien seeking a new home for his people on Earth. He is Hercules. The man standing behind him is Herzog.

One year at Telluride, Herzog invited me up to his room in the New Sheridan Hotel to show me the VHS tape of his newest film, *Bells from the Deep*. It was about the people of a small village in Russia that stands on the bank of a lake. These people believe that at the bottom of the lake there is a city inhabited by angels. You can only see it on a few days every year when the ice is thin enough to see through, but not so thin they would crash in and drown.

Foot by foot, inch by inch, the villagers creep forward on the ice. They hear obscure groaning and moanings as the ice complains. Sometime a crack shoots out from them and they freeze, unsure whether to continue. Eagerly they peer into the ice, seeking the faces of the angels.

I don't believe the film was ever released, perhaps because it lacked closure. The village people saw the angel city, and none of them drowned.

"That must have been you with a camera crawling on the ice behind them," I said.

"I would not ask anyone to take a chance I would not take myself," he said.

Then he told me that there was no village and he made the whole story up. I remember him at Cannes, after the premiere of *Where the Green Ants Dream* (1984). At the press conference, a journalist from Australia asked him the source for his information about Aboriginal beliefs. "There is no source," he said. "They made up their beliefs, and I made up mine."

For that matter, *Little Dieter Needs to Fly* (1997), a documentary based on the life of a man locked up for years in a Laotian prison camp, opens with a sequence in which the man arrives home and compulsively opens every door, cupboard, and drawer in his house many times, to be sure they're not locked. All made up. That doc was remade into *Rescue Dawn*, which centers on a jungle trek consisting of Dieter's escape on a journey that had its details largely invented.

When Herzog made *The White Diamond* (2004), he was again determined to take the chances himself. That was his documentary about Dorrington, the naturalist who believed there were forms of life living in the canopy of the rain forest that were born, lived, and died without ever touching the earth. Because the fragile growth at that height will not permit climbing, Dorrington constructed the White Diamond, a teardrop-shaped airship with an open gondola, which would be lifted by a balloon to deliver the Diamond into the trees, where it could gingerly investigate the creatures he expected to find there.

Dorrington tested an earlier airship in 1993 in Sumatra, and that ended with catastrophe. His cinematographer, Dieter Plage, fell from the gondola after it was broken on the high branches of a tree by a sudden wind. "It was an accident," says Dorrington, and all agree, but he blames himself every day. Now he is ready to try again.

Before the first test flight, Herzog has an argument with Dorrington. The scientist wants to fly solo. Herzog calls it "stupid" that the first flight might take place without a camera on board. It might be the only flight. Herzog brought along two cinematographers but insists he must personally take the camera up on the maiden voyage. "I cannot ask a cinematographer to get in an airship before I test it myself," he says.

Up they go, the two men dangling in the teardrop. There are some dicey moments when the ship goes backward when it should go forward, and Herzog observes a motor burning out and pieces of a propeller whizzing past his head. The ship skims the forest canopy before it descends to dip a toe in the river.

Mournful, ecclesiastical music accompanies these images. The vast Kaieteur Falls fascinates the party; its waters are golden-brown as they roar into a maelstrom, while countless swifts and other birds fly into a cave behind the curtain of water. Mark Anthony Yhap, a Rastafarian employed by the expedition, tells them legends about the cave. The team doctor, Michael Wilk, has himself lowered on a rope with a video camera to look into the cave. It is typical of a Herzog project that the doctor would be "an experienced mountain climber." It is sublimely typical that Herzo doesn't show us the doctor's footage of the cave, after Yhap argues that its sacred secrets must be preserved. What is in the cave? A lot of guano, is my guess.

Herzog insists to the universe: *Sir, I exist!* Another year at Telluride, he and his small team had just returned after a failed shoot on top of a mountain. It was a clear day but a freak storm blew up and buried them in snow. They dug themselves out and climbed back down.

Herzog is three months younger than I am. His people and my German relatives are from Munich. It isn't impossible that we're distant cousins. The first time I met him was at somebody's apartment in Greenwich Village during the New York Film Festival. I sat on the rug at his feet. What we talked about I have no idea, but I felt a strong connection and I've felt it ever since. He was a kid with a film at the festival, yet so much more than that.

Other kids like him have grown up to make blockbusters and command millions of dollars for budgets, but Herzog has never wavered. He has made the films he chooses, as he chooses, and now at seventy and with forty-seven directorial credits, he has never made a film to be ashamed of. How he finances them I do not know, but it's not from the profits of his previous films. Asked what he would do if told the world were ending tomorrow, he said, "Martin Luther said he would plant a tree. I would start a film."

One year he came to Ebertfest and told us his journey to Urbana began on top of a plateau in South America, from which he had himself lowered by ropes down the side, and trekked with tribesmen to a river where a dugout canoe took him to a city with a steamship. One of the Far-Flung Correspondents told me: "He wouldn't have come otherwise. It was the difficulty that made it irresistible."

Everybody knows the story of how, in November 1974, Herzog learned that the great German cineaste Lotte Eisner was near death at seventy-eight. A survivor of the Nazi camps, she had settled in Paris and helped found the Cinémathèque Française. During World War II she was interned in a Nazi camp. After the war she worked closely with Henri Langlois, founder of the Cinémathèque Française, as the chief archivist. Carrying a backpack and wearing new boots, Herzog walked from Munich to her bedside.

Werner Herzog wrote in his journal, "This must not be, not at this time; German cinema could not do without her now." So, in a gesture of iron-willed control over apparently dark inevitability, Herzog decided to walk from his home in Munich to Paris to visit Eisner, convinced that if he did so, she would recover. Herzog set off on what will be a three-week odyssey equipped with land backpack and a new pair of boots. John Bailey of the American Society of Cinematographers wrote in the ASC journal: "Herzog's confrontation with the raw elements of an early winter and its assault on his body reads as an analogue for that of many of his fictional characters, who also face down and are battered by implacable if not outright hostile Nature. Neither Aguirre, Fitzcarraldo, nor Dieter Dengler lives in a time and space continuum much different from that which Herzog faced on this journey. If the sheer physical discomfort he endured—from rain, ice, snow, chilling wind, suspicious peasants and farmer—were a measure of grace gained, then Lotte Eisner, who died in 1983 at 87, would still be alive."

Herzog is open to less noble challenges. When he was living in Berkeley in the 1970s, the Telluride cofounder Tom Luddy introduced him to a young man named Errol Morris, who was making *Gates of Heaven*, a feature documentary about a pet cemetery. "If you finish that film, I will eat my shoe," Herzog told him. Morris finished the film and Herzog ate his shoe. Luddy was running the Pacific Film Archive at the time and arranged for Herzog to eat his shoe onstage after it had been made more palatable by Alice Waters, of Chez Panisse. I recall hot sauce and bay leaves.

Herzog's new film *Happy People: A Year in the Taiga* is a new unfolding of his life in search of the extremes. Having made *Encounters at the End of the World* (2007), about the occupants of a research station at the South Pole, wasn't it inevitable for him to turn to those who live in Siberia, inside the Arctic Circle? These hunters and trappers in a village of about four hundred live off the land with their own hands and resources. The first generation was set down there by the Soviet

Communist government and directed to hunt, fish, and trap for fur. The airlift didn't return on schedule, and they lived in an unheated hut, with no winter clothing, no firewood, and hardly any tools. One of the survivors of that time tells the camera that one of the early settlers "didn't make it. I guess he didn't have what it takes."

The film is divided reasonably into winter, spring, summer, and autumn. Each season is triggered to prepare for the next. In early autumn they're knocking on trees to dislodge nuts for their winter meals. Their nets capture pike that will be salted away. They use moss and other insulations to weatherproof their cottages. They aren't entirely without modern equipment; we see chainsaws, steel axes and hatchets, outboard engines, and motorbikes. They wear modern outdoor clothing. In this land where everything is stretched taut, one man allows himself the luxury of cigarettes.

The film pays close attention to what they do and how they do it. They hollow and shape a log of just the right size for a dugout canoe, use wedges to push its sides apart, and fix it in shape with fire. They make tar from tree bark to caulk it. They slice wood from the sides of trees and construct their skis. They use smaller trees to set their spring-loaded animal traps, hundreds of traps for each man. In their hands a steel hatchet reduces each tree to their needs, and we reflect that technology like stone axes, wooden wedges, and levers were used by our earliest ancestors. We learn how they're able to avoid carving the sides of a dugout too thin. How they shave, soften, and shape their skis. How they paint themselves with tar to repel the clouds of mosquitoes. How their lives entwine with the lives of sables.

The people of the taiga speak to the camera and are used in voice-over as they explain how and why they do things. Herzog adds his own narration, a mixture of measured explanation, wonder, and the implacable nature of what is being described. Steven Boone, who wrote this acutely observant review of *Happy People* on my website, calls it The Voice: "The films could probably stand on their own merits without That Voice, but why should they?" Boone describes the men of the taiga: "They live off the land and are self-reliant, truly free. No rules, no taxes, no government, no laws, no bureaucracy, no phones, no radio, equipped only with their individual values and standard of conduct." The Voice has no tones for sentimentality.

One element of *Happy People* struck me. My DVD had to skip over a "damaged area" and I may have missed them, but I recall no women in the film. How can that be? There are children. The great undiscovered continent of the Herzogian cinema is the female gender. They're there—but serving supporting roles. It is not that he avoids strong, talented women. His wife Lena is a Russian-born photographer who works for major publications, has gallery shows, and has published four books of her work.

The "codirector" of *Happy People* is a Russian cinematographer named Dmitry Vasyukov. It didn't surprise me to learn that Herzog himself wasn't in Siberia to shoot the footage. He was shown four hours of it by a friend in Los Angeles, and determined to edit and narrate the material. His film focuses uncompromisingly on these men and their lives and subscribes adamantly to how he in *Fitzcarraldo* describes Nature: "Overwhelming and collective murder."

He made at least one other film edited mostly from someone else's work: the great success *Grizzly Man* (2005). Timothy Treadwell lived among the grizzlies in Alaska every summer for years until one autumn a bear attacked him and his girlfriend, killed them, and ate them. In his narration for that film, Herzog says: "And what haunts me, is that in all the faces of all the bears that Treadwell ever filmed, I discover no kinship, no understanding, no mercy. I see only the overwhelming indifference of nature. To me, there is no such thing as a secret world of the bears. And this blank stare speaks only of a half-bored interest in food. But for Timothy Treadwell, this bear was a friend, a savior."

I believe Herzog has a conviction that our civilization teeters on the brink of collapse, and that those who live may have to do so by their wills and skills. If global warming takes its toll, the people of the taiga will be well-located and equipped to survive. They will be even happier when it's summertime, and the livin' is easy.

Appendix

Note concerning Herzog's Films

Prepared February 1999 for a retrospective at the Walker Art Center, Minneapolis, Minnesota, April 2–May 1, 1999

One day at the Cannes Film Festival, I was sitting in a cafe with Werner Herzog and he told me, "Our civilization is starving for great images." I walked out of the café and into a screening and saw shots of people driving in cars and sitting in restaurants; the camera cut back and forth as they talked with each other about sex and crime, and I thought, yes, he's right, these are not the images that will nourish us.

In Herzog's films you will see monkeys gibbering around a madman in armor, who is on a sinking raft on the Amazon. And a man standing on a mountaintop and seeing the future. Villagers stunned with grief, breaking beer steins over each other's heads because the secret of rose-colored glass has been lost. A man dragging a ship overland through the jungle. People creeping out onto thin ice to see the angels in a city at the bottom of a lake. A chicken going around and around on a conveyor belt. Clouds pouring like water down into a valley. A vampire in his grave of flesh. A man opening and closing every door in his house again and again, to be sure he is not locked in. A stagehand backstage at an opera, joyfully singing along with the tenor. A man locked in a cellar for years, wandering in amazement in the open air. The Jesuses of Russia, in sandals and beards, walking across the land with their gospel—each one presenting himself as the Christ. Dwarves in revolt. A man who could ski jump so well he was always in danger of overshooting the landing area and flying on and on to his death. A ghost town in the shadow of a volcano expected to explode at any moment. A message being passed in a human chain reaching across the hills. This list could continue indefinitely. Some of these images are from documentaries, some are from fiction; can you guess which ones?

I met Herzog at the New York Film Festival, where he had shown his film *Signs of Life*, which Bob Shaye chose to inaugurate his new company New Line Cinema. We sat in Shaye's little apartment on Washington Square and talked into the night about the liberating, transforming power of the cinema. Every time I have seen Herzog since, the conversation has continued. Here is a man with a sublime indifference to the currents of ordinary commercial cinema. His films feel seized with visions. His characters dream of transcendence.

I think of him like those people creeping out of the ice. Each of his projects is precariously financed, because he does not supply explosions and people driving around in cars and smoking cigarettes in diners while engaged in sub-Tarantino wit about sex and crime. He doesn't have the knack of being conventional. He is looking for the angels in their city. Maybe he will see them at last, and show them to us. Maybe the ice will break and he will drown. Or, drowning, sink down, down to be saved by the angels.

Herzog's "Minnesota Declaration"

Presented April 30, 1999, by Werner Herzog at a question-and-answer session with Roger Ebert at the Walker Art Center, Minneapolis; often referred to as the "Minnesota Declaration."

Lessons of Darkness
Minnesota declaration: truth and fact in documentary cinema

1. By dint of declaration the so-called Cinema Verité is devoid of verité. It reaches a merely superficial truth, the truth of accountants.
2. One well-known representative of Cinema Verité declared publicly

that truth can be easily found by taking a camera and trying to be honest. He resembles the night watchman at the Supreme Court who resents the amount of written law and legal procedures. "For me," he says, "there should be only one single law: the bad guys should go to jail."

Unfortunately, he is part right, for most of the many, much of the time.

3. Cinema Verité confounds fact and truth, and thus plows only stones. And yet, facts sometimes have a strange and bizarre power that makes their inherent truth seem unbelievable.

4. Fact creates norms, and truth illumination.

5. There are deeper strata of truth in cinema, and there is such a thing as poetic, ecstatic truth. It is mysterious and elusive, and can be reached only through fabrication and imagination and stylization.

6. Filmmakers of Cinema Verité resemble tourists who take pictures of ancient ruins of facts.

7. Tourism is sin, and travel on foot virtue.

8. Each year at springtime scores of people on snowmobiles crash through the melting ice on the lakes of Minnesota and drown. Pressure is mounting on the new governor to pass a protective law. He, the former wrestler and bodyguard, has the only sage answer to this: "You can't legislate stupidity."

9. The gauntlet is hereby thrown down.

10. The moon is dull. Mother Nature doesn't call, doesn't speak to you, although a glacier eventually farts. And don't you listen to the Song of Life.

11. We ought to be grateful that the Universe out there knows no smile.

12. Life in the oceans must be sheer hell. A vast, merciless hell of permanent and immediate danger. So much of hell that during evolution some species — including man — crawled, fled onto some small continents of solid land, where the *Lessons of Darkness* continue.

Index